Ordinary Heroes

A Future for Men

ORDINARY HEROES

A Future for Men

Michael Hardiman

Newleaf

Newleaf
an imprint of
Gill & Macmillan Ltd
Goldenbridge
Dublin 8
with associated companies throughout the world
www.gillmacmillan.ie

0 7171 2934 9

Design and print origination by
O'K Graphic Design, Dublin

Printed by
ColourBooks Ltd, Dublin

This book is typeset in 10/14 pt Garamond Book

A CIP catalogue record for this book is available from the British Library.

1 3 5 4 2

For my father, James Hardiman, and for the blessings in knowing him

Contents

Introduction

Most personal development books are written by women, bought by women and read by women. This trend suggests that women are more interested in the nature of emotional development and in the pursuit of mental health. Women, it seems, are also more likely to acknowledge if they have a problem on the one hand and more ready to accept help on the other. Men are far more reluctant to engage in efforts at self-discovery. Many view the need for self-understanding and personal development as a sign of weakness and some perhaps fear what they will find if they take the time to explore their inner world. As a consequence there is an imbalance between the sexes in relation to using the information currently available concerning psychological development and emotional health. Men are being left even further behind when it comes to getting the information they need to pursue healthier lives. This reality has serious consequences for men's health as well as for the functioning of society as a whole.

Our postmodern, consumer-oriented social system brings many benefits but also contains many flaws and dangers. It is a society that is largely promoted and executed by men. Kate Millet is eloquent in her assertion that

> our society, like all other historical civilisations, is a patriarchy. The fact is evident at once if one recalls that the military, industry, technology, universitics, science, political office and finance — in short, every avenue of power

> within society, including the coercive power of the police — is entirely in male hands. As the essence of politics is power, such realisation cannot fail to carry impact . . . If one takes patriarchal government to be the institution whereby that half of the populace which is female is controlled by that half which is male, the principles of patriarchy appear twofold: male shall dominate female, elder male shall dominate younger.

While some changes have occurred since Millet wrote this in 1970 the essence of her description remains true. Men, to a large extent, still rule the world. Men of goodwill who in many cases truly believe that they are doing it right. Men who themselves are being eroded, often unconsciously, by their commitment to and zeal for what Kenneth Clark calls a 'heroic materialism'.

Most men do not know how they are contributing to the problems of modern society. Rather, most of us cannot see that each of us is a link in a chain, and that each person bears some responsibility, however small, for the structure and behaviour of the group as a whole. I believe that most men are unaware that their way of functioning in the world has been compromised from their earliest days, and that their health and safety has always been a disposable commodity. In the battle for human survival up into this century, men have paid with their lives, their souls and their hearts. In general, men have been encouraged and rewarded for developing and using their minds and their bodies because problem solving and physical labour are useful coinage in the currency of affluent materialism. What they have lost, or never been allowed to develop, is what is often mistakenly called their feminine side. Sensitivity, affection, nurturing and feelings are not feminine qualities. They are human qualities that are often seen as feminine because they are less apparent in men. The inhibition of these aspects of development has created a serious imbalance in the way that men experience their lives and in the way they live and behave. When the effect of this imbalance is seen on a global scale it makes much sense of the way that modern society has evolved.

For many reasons, mothers and fathers have colluded through the ages to prevent men developing as balanced human beings. They have done this often in ignorance, sometimes in good faith and in most cases as a result of cultural taboos and social pressure. And yet it is the task and challenge for modern men who wish to be fully human to reclaim their lost inheritance, and to break the moulds that compromised so many spiritually and emotionally, before they had the choice or the voice to prevent it.

This book is an attempt to address this imbalance by presenting guidance and information related to emotional health for men in a manner that is particularly relevant to them as they live their lives in present-day society. I will refer quite a bit to modern films, television, stories and other popular art forms as well as to the insights that I have been privileged to reach through working with men as they come to terms with the challenge of evolving into more balanced and self-aware people. These areas and my own personal experiences of maturing and coming to terms with understanding masculinity seem to express much that is of relevance to the predicaments that men face. I hope this book will explain some of the more difficult conundrums facing men who want to grow and change, and who know at the deepest level that they are being prostituted to a world which will use them up and then discard them.

PART ONE

Formative Influences in Becoming a Man

1 The Making of a Man

Introduction

This chapter explores some of the crucial elements that influence the formation of men. These influences are responsible, to a large extent, for the way that men operate in the world. They shape the beliefs men have about manhood and masculinity, and they affect the ways men relate to each other, to women and to children. They also play a significant part in developing men's attitudes to work and its place in the scheme of things. The discussion here is brief because there are several excellent works by eminent men such as Sam Keen, Warren Farrell and Robert Bly that are devoted solely to this topic. These and other authors provide rich and sometimes poetic descriptions of the history of men and their evolution to the present day. I am grateful for their influences on my own formation and thinking. This chapter is an outline of some of the key areas that I believe underlie much of the dysfunctional and unhealthy patterns that afflict a great number of modern men.

Men are suffering

The evidence is accumulating that men are in serious trouble. The following statistical profile from the United States is very revealing. When we take an overall view of the destructive aspects that are apparent in the modern world we see that men feature very powerfully as both the agents and the victims. Some particularly relevant statistics in this regard are presented by Warren Farrell in his provocative book *The Myth of Male Power*.

His research is based on trends in the United States but I have no reason to believe that they are not reflected in a similar fashion in Western Europe.

- Men die earlier than women from all fifteen of the leading causes of death.
- Men are four times more likely than women to develop heart disease by the age of fifty.
- Almost all premature deaths in men after the first year can be related to stress-induced conditions or behaviour, from suicides to heart attacks, from cancer to murder.
- No governmental agency focusing on health spends as much on men's health as on women's health. In the United Kingdom it is estimated that six times more money is spent on women's health.
- Of the roughly 275,000 homeless people in the United States 83 per cent are men.
- Of the roughly one million prisoners in the United States 94 per cent are men.
- Men are ten times more likely to commit suicide after the death of a spouse than are women.
- Ninety-four per cent of occupational deaths happen to men.
- In Ireland young men (under thirty-five) are seven times more likely to commit suicide than are women.

What do these findings tell us about men? In brief, men are more physically and emotionally vulnerable to disease, injury, alienation and violence. After a generation of discussion about the need for equality there remain some serious inequalities and not all of these disenfranchise women. It is the aspiration of all evolved and humane societies to uphold the ideal that human beings are created equal. We must ask ourselves then why have men paid such a high price for being male. It is my opinion that much male suffering, especially the alienation, loneliness and frustration that is so eloquently described by Terrence Real in his book *I Don't Want to Talk About It: Overcoming the Secret Legacy of Male Depression*, is a direct consequence of men trying to express their masculinity in ways that have become outmoded and dangerous to their health and happiness. To examine why these trends are so clearly developing we must first look at the nature of manhood.

What is a man?

One of the most common assumptions about the human race is that people have single unchangeable natures. Most people think that human beings are moulded by the genetic code that determines their shape, size, sex and personality. To some extent this belief is accurate. Human beings reflect a range of possible variations of size, shape, colour, intelligence and temperament. Certain aspects of these differences are determined by the unique genetic code in each individual. Almost all other aspects of the way people behave, the jobs they choose, the people they are attracted to, religious beliefs, capacity for love and intimacy, their use of aggression and so on, are heavily influenced by learning and early experience. This means that most of what is dysfunctional and unhealthy about men in today's world is learned behaviour that has its roots in their social and family upbringing. While the focus of this chapter is concerned with those aspects of becoming a man that are learned, and thus can be changed, some brief discussion of the physical elements of masculinity is relevant.

The biology of manhood

Men have specific biological characteristics that define them as male. They share these with the males of most higher order mammals in the animal kingdom. In general, males are bigger and physically more powerful than females, while females have greater physical endurance. They are more aggressive and experience a more urgent and immediate sex drive, that is initially triggered by cues such as sight and smell. Male social interactions and the structure of their groupings are heavily influenced by the issue of dominance. These characteristics seem to be a direct result of far higher levels of the hormone testosterone that, in the case of humans and higher primates, is programmed via genetic make-up to announce its presence *in utero* and shapes the male differently from the female. These differences have long been noted, and go some way to explain the behaviours and interactions between males and females in the animal kingdom. Such biological differences are insubstantial in explaining the radical differences that seem to exist between men and women when it comes to the issue of psychological and mental functioning. These differences have been minimised in recent decades as part of an ideological battle that occurred as a result of the growth of feminism as a force for social change. Feminist influence has, to a large extent, been reluctant to acknowledge gender differences, arguing that all but the most obvious and visible differences are a result of cultural and social training rather than a result of genetic make-up. Accordingly, most of the differences could be erased by changes to child rearing practices and equal rights legislation. In this view men and women are, in fact, very alike but are taught, by their social environment, to be different.

Recent research has undermined the naivety implicit in this position. Studies that use the highly sophisticated technological advances in brain scanning and investigations show that there are significant differences between men and women that cannot be simply reduced to the influence of learning. Certain examples are particularly telling in this regard. The male brain differs somewhat from the female. Language centres are more discrete in men. The bridge between the intuitive artistic side of the brain and the logical side is smaller in men than in women, meaning that there is less communication between these two aspects of brain function in men. Men are more likely to get a joke that they hear in their left ear (processing it by way of the right brain, i.e. the logical side), women more likely to get a joke heard through the right ear (i.e. processing it in the left brain). Women are more likely to be right-handed. These and other findings have given scientific validity to the argument that men and women have subtle differences in the way they think. In turn, these findings can be used to support many of the not so politically correct clichés such as: men are logical and reasoning whereas women are emotional and intuitive; men are silent and withdrawn, women are talkative and expressive; women are nurturing and relationship-oriented, men are problem-focused and practical. Brain research also provides some explanations for the long-known facts that, in general, little girls learn language faster, and that boys are better in general at spatial reasoning (chess playing, for example). Baby girls are more attracted to faces than are boys, who are more likely to show interest in patterns.

These findings have led to a variety of theories about communication between men and women, such as the hugely popular notions expressed in John Gray's works. He has coined the phrase 'Men are from Mars and women are from Venus' as a way of describing the effects that neurological differences have on the way men and women deal with their world and more specifically how they deal with each other. The fundamental differences between the sexes, if not understood by both men and women, can in his view lead to all kinds of difficulties in communication, as well as high levels of relationship breakdown.

What is clear from all of this is that if we are to try to understand the role of men in today's world we need to take into account the inheritance of male characteristics as well as the events that shape men in their early social environment. When we take these two aspects as a combination of influences we discover some very important information about what makes men the way they are, and how well they can adjust to and function in the modern world. Let us look at the genetic inheritance issue first.

Genetic influences

With regard to the first area the history of the humble moth has a story to tell us that might be of value in this discussion. Before the Industrial Revolution one particular species of moth (the peppered moth) was quite common. The vast majority of these moths were pale in colour, a variety of different shades from white to yellow, with small dark specks. A dark moth was a rare sight, easily picked out against the wall of a house, a leaf or a flower. As the industrial machinery expanded, bigger factories were built and huge coal-driven furnaces pumped out vast quantities of smoke which gradually discoloured and darkened the walls of buildings, trees and the environment as a whole. Within a few years there were very few light-coloured moths to be found and yet the numbers of moths stayed roughly the same. How did this happen? Very simply, the moths that were darker, which were originally easily spotted by the preying birds, now had an advantage, whereas the light-coloured moths were eaten up with relish. Now more of the darker moths lived long enough to reproduce and the gene that produced darker wings spread swiftly in the gene pool. This process is called natural selection and refers to the principle that if some characteristic has an advantage for the survival of an animal then it is more likely to be carried on into the next generation. With creatures that reproduce quickly it is easier to see this principle at work. With complex animals and human beings it is difficult to see these changes because the lifespans are longer. Perhaps some of the differences being noticed between men and women are a result of this kind of process.

A simple example in my own experience suggests this to be the case. One of my uncles was born the elder son in a family of seven, with a brother and five sisters. Thomas was a sensitive, intelligent child with a love for nature, an aversion to physical labour and a love for female company. He grew up on a small farm, in a rural townland peopled by men and women who were strict, hard-working and intolerant of difference. Thomas became an outcast of sorts who developed into a charming rebel, a likeable rogue, who told stories and drank a lot. All efforts to match him in marriage failed and he died relatively young. The genetic profile that gave him much of his sensitivity died with him. It died with him and with countless other men because it was not considered valuable to his society and while it could charm a woman it would not feed her children. Is it possible that gradually over hundreds of generations the male gene pool became poorer in the qualities that we now refer to as feminine, and richer in those that guaranteed physical survival? Perhaps the hard, focused, aggressive and competitive men, strong and brave warriors and long-suffering workers physically able to withstand the elements were selected at the cost of those more sensitive and intuitive and less physically able.

More recently I had several discussions with a female client that illustrate this issue further. She had much difficulty in finding a suitable male partner. By this she meant meeting a man who was not bedevilled by problems. Most of her relationships were with men who would suit the case histories in the self-help books that stereotype troubled men, best-sellers such as *Women who Love Too Much*, *Men who Hate Women and the Women who Love Them* and *Smart Women, Foolish Choices*, to mention just a few. She herself was a passionate and creative person, deeply emotional as well as radical in her thinking. I asked her about the kinds of men she was attracted to and with whom she would like to spend time. She described her preferred male as someone who was emotional, interested in the complexities of life, creative and independent.

As she described her preferences she realised that all the relationships she had with men were with men who reflected these qualities, but they were also very troubled and inadequate to the tasks of financial security, consistent parenting and a lot else. They were angry, drank too much and continually seemed to be in some sort of internal strife. As we continued our analysis of these men, she concluded that the reason so many of them were troubled and struggling was that the very qualities she liked were also those that left them on the margins of society. They drank too much to cope with rejection, they couldn't hold down jobs that required no creativity. They were not prepared to suffer alienation from themselves in return for some ego stroking about their value to a company or group. In turn, they suffered more than most and paid a high price for trying to be the men they wanted to be in a world that wanted something else. She believed, and I am inclined to agree with her, that men who reflected the qualities she wanted were not going to be found in the mainstream of society. Most would have much more difficult lives than those who engaged in the power struggles for achievement, who defined their worth by financial success and who sold their intellectual or physical resources to the highest bidder.

Taking these stories together we can reach a very important insight in our understanding of the forces that shape men. It is unnecessary to accept that the predominance of certain characteristics of men is a biological given, to be tolerated or considered intrinsic to being male. They may simply be the long-term outcome of generations of natural selection. Some of the very characteristics that once were helpful to the survival of the human race have become hindrances to men's healthy functioning in the modern world. There is a strong case to be made that our traditional notions of how men should act and behave is no longer useful and is causing great suffering and turmoil in the lives of men.

If we change our definition of what it means to be male then maybe we will see in future generations a broader and more varied kind of male emerging. This is, of course, cold comfort to the many men who are going to die young of stress-related illness, or those who cannot cope with not being good enough or tough enough and who will kill themselves either dramatically through suicide or more slowly through addiction and self-abuse. It is of little value to these and others to suggest that by changing our definition of men today we will create a different possibility for men in a thousand years time. Thankfully, making changes today can have more immediate results in the day-to-day life experience of men, but it will be in spite of rather than with the aid of their genetic and neurological programming. To change our definition of what it means to be a successful healthy man we need firstly to examine the way society, through the family and other institutions, shapes masculinity.

Early childhood experiences

Early childhood experience is the second strand in the cable of male development. Certain early influences seem to have an impact on the make-up of the male brain. Let us look at what happens to the brain after birth. We now know that the brain of a newborn child is developed only in those areas that are needed to guarantee survival, namely those that regulate breathing, blood circulation and digestion. The human brain differs in many respects from those of our nearest relatives in the animal kingdom. A particularly striking difference lies in the fact that, at birth, the human brain weighs only 25 per cent of its fully mature weight where our nearest relatives have brains that weigh approximately 50 to 60 per cent of adult weight at birth. In humans many areas are undeveloped and await the influence of environmental stimulation in order to begin building the enormously complex structure that is the mature brain. The architecture of the structure that emerges will be influenced by the kinds of experiences to which the child is exposed. In simple terms this means that if boys are treated differently from girls in their early years there will be subtle but important differences in brain functioning. The implications here are, of course, very significant and wide-ranging for understanding how men and women become the way they are.

To clarify the issue a bit further let us look at what happens to the brain during the development of language. As the infant hears the sounds of words being spoken certain groups of brain cells (neurons) assign themselves to certain sounds. Within a period of two to three years most of the sounds in the language of the infant have brain cells devoted to them. When that particular sound enters the ear and is sent through the auditory nerve to the brain the neurons fire in response and the child recognises the sound or group of sounds that make up a word. The brain has created a map or web of nerve cells organised around a particular language. In a different language the sounds are different and a different structure emerges. By the age of five most of the nerve cells have been assigned and are not available to new sounds. This means that new languages will be difficult to learn and, more specifically, languages that use very different types of sounds will become next to impossible. Children deprived of hearing spoken language through deafness will, if cured later than the age of five or six years, in most cases never be able to speak fluently. Furthermore, and more interestingly from the point of view of the present discussion, there are different areas of brain function that develop in a similar fashion right throughout childhood; these include motor development, vision, emotional control, social attachment, maths and logic, and music. There are profound implications here, which have yet to be researched, for the way that men and women may be shaped differently. Of particular significance may be the way that the emotional centres develop through experiences of consistent affection and expressions of feelings.

A recent event brought this especially close to my attention. I was attending a religious ceremony. It involved a special confirmation mass which lasted over an hour. Because confirmation is very much a family occasion there were many children in attendance. The hour-long ceremony is for most children (and some adults) very boring. A family of a mother and four children sat in the pew in front of me. The children ranged in age from about eleven down to two years of age. The youngest child, a boy with big brown eyes, intrigued me. He did what little boys do, explored and crawled around under seats, pretended to shoot the youngster in the pew in front of him. Every now and then he returned to his mother's lap. He sat facing her and, like a blind man reading Braille, he explored the contours of her face with his little hands. His gaze into her eyes was constant and full of warmth. He snuggled into her and ran his lips on her hair and face. He seemed totally engrossed in the sensuous delight of his mother. She reciprocated throughout what for me seemed a long time so overtaken was I at the simple beauty of the scene. Then, completely filled up with the smells, taste, feel and look of his mother (and his first love), he returned to playing and exploring the surroundings.

Watching this scene I reflected on the complete ease and familiarity the two had with each other, and realised that it was most likely a feature of their attachment from his infancy. And as his little brain was making its map of the world it had created a special treasure chest for this kind of affectionate love. Unless some extraordinary harm comes to this young child in his development into manhood he will be able to savour the delights of sensual experiences as well as intimate sexual love in adulthood. This simple example holds a great truth: the men we become are shaped not just from inherited genes but also from our earliest childhood experiences.

Summary

This chapter examined a fundamental starting point in our understanding of what makes men the way they are. Generation upon generation of selecting and rewarding certain kinds of ways of being a man leads to a strengthening of a genetic bias in those directions. On top of this genetic bias there is the effect of early childhood experiences that guides and further strengthens the individual to become what his society defines as the model of masculinity. The evidence suggests that as a result of these shaping experiences many men are now suffering a plethora of disorders as they try to cope with the demands of modern society for which it appears they are ill-equipped. The model of masculinity that has been encouraged through these influences is examined in the next chapter.

2 The Shaping of Manhood

Introduction

All people are shaped to some extent by their early environment in both family and society. Some resistance to this idea still exists but, in my view, those who cannot accept this are acting from the point of view of prejudice rather than rational sense. The earth is not flat even though, for a great proportion of human history, most people believed it to be so! Human beings are not completely rational or completely free. Rather we are living our lives in ways that have been profoundly influenced by early messages imprinted on our minds and often out of conscious awareness. Those who stay unaware of the forces that shape them remain prisoners to these influences, and often live out lives that are not truly their own but simply a script written by someone else.

Others who learn about the forces that affected them during their formation can gain a high degree of control over them and experience true freedom, namely an ability to shape one's own life. All of this is true of men and women. The influences that are brought to bear are, however, different. What is of special interest in this discussion is that men are shaped in particular ways from the very earliest days of life. And if men are to understand themselves, the challenges they face, and their needs regarding health and fulfilment then they need to become aware of these influences.

A personal incident comes to mind. When my mother was

pregnant with her first child, my grandparents were greatly excited. My father's father was especially moved because my father was the only male in his family that was married and likely to carry the family name into the next generation. His other son, my uncle Thomas, was for reasons mentioned above unlikely to marry. As the time came for my mother to give birth my grandfather spent the day in church praying for a safe delivery. While delighted to hear the news that the baby was born healthy and the mother well, he was crestfallen to find out that my mother had delivered a baby girl. On her next pregnancy he was even more intent with his prayers and came to the house full of trepidation to be relieved and overjoyed at the news of my birth. He now had a grandson who was named after him. He had been ill for some time and he died a few months after my birth. I believe that he waited for that event before he could die in peace.

On the surface this story can be seen to reflect an undervaluing of women, a favouring of boys, as well as a simplistic view of life. Another way of looking at it is to see it as representing the widely held belief at that time, that men are responsible for providing for and protecting the human family, and that without a male heir to take over responsibilities the gains carved out by a man's life of toil and suffering against the elements and forces of nature would all be for naught. Whichever way we look at this event it does reflect a reality that, for good or ill, from the moment of birth, there were different expectations and beliefs about the place, roles and value of men and women. These expectations continued on throughout childhood shaping the children into the moulds created in the minds of their parents and society at large.

Key elements in cultivating and forming men

It is an enormous task to examine any aspect of human development. To undertake one such as understanding the way men are formed is perhaps impossible without making serious compromises and setting important limitations. For the sake of this book I will limit myself to the areas of general beliefs about men that have wide acceptance in Western culture, and the means by which these beliefs are processed through family systems. In all of this it is important to note that I examine this issue from a position of being a male white middle-class educated psychologist with his own influential developmental history. If I were an African-American civil rights campaigner, or a Puerto Rican illegal immigrant, working in a sweatshop in Chicago, or a mother of five living with an alcoholic in a tenement, I'm sure that my opinions and beliefs about men, as well as my analysis of their nature, would be different.

Feminist philosopher Susan Bordo makes this point eloquently in relation to feminist interpretation of history.

> We also need to guard against the 'view from nowhere' supposition that if we only employ the right method we can avoid ethnocentrism, totalizing constructions, and false universalizations. No matter how local and circumscribed the object or how attentive the scholar is to the axes that constitute social identity, some of those axes will be ignored and others selected. This is an inescapable fact of human embodiment, as Nietzsche was the first to point out: 'The eye . . . in which the active and interpreting forces, through which alone seeing becomes seeing *something*, are supposed to be lacking is an absurdity and a nonsense. There is *only* perspectival seeing, *only* a perspectival knowing.' This selectivity, moreover, is never innocent. We always 'see' from points of view that are invested with our social, political, and personal interests, inescapably-centric in one way or another . . .

Bias is therefore unavoidable in the nature of a work such as this. The best one can hope for is a commitment to objectivity and open-mindedness. Having set out these parameters let us examine some of the key themes that are unconsciously at work in moulding men from their earliest days of life. In my opinion there are at least three fundamental beliefs at work in the collective unconscious of Western societies that determine their expectations and treatment of men. These expectations and beliefs have, in my opinion, been essential aspects of the survival of the human family thus far, but also have led to much unnecessary suffering. Additionally, some of these influences are no longer valuable to the kind of societies we have now and many men are left bereft and troubled as they try to live out their own individual lives with some modicum of health and happiness. Three themes emerge from my analysis of the expectations and influences that have shaped men for recent human history. These are as follows:

(i) Men are expected to sacrifice themselves.
(ii) Men are expected to protect and provide for women.
(iii) Men are valued only in terms of what they can achieve.

The enormous developments that lie at the foundation of modern Western society, namely technology, engineering, communication, health care, recreation, economic security and so on, are, in my opinion, the direct result of large numbers of men responding, often unconsciously, to the demands inherent in these beliefs. Furthermore I believe that the enormous levels of suffering brought about through male violence and through self-destructive behaviour are a direct result of large numbers of men being unable or unwilling to cope with these unspoken demands. Let us look at the implications of each.

(i) Men are expected to sacrifice themselves

When we look beneath the surface of the statistics that show how vulnerable men are to early death through stress-related diseases, violence and lack of adequate self-care, we see a theme. Somewhere along the line men have learned to sacrifice their health and well-being. There are many examples in the literature of mythology and religion that deal with this theme. Perhaps the most lucid one is presented in the biblical story of Abraham and Isaac. I will use this as a foundation for a discussion of this aspect of male development. Let us first repeat the story as presented in Genesis, chapter 22.

> Some time after these events, God put Abraham to the test. He called to him 'Abraham!' 'Ready,' he replied. Then God said: 'Take your son Isaac, your only one, whom you love, and go into the land of Moriah. There you shall offer him up as a burnt offering on a height that I will point out to you.' Early the next morning Abraham saddled his donkey, took with him his son Isaac and two servants as well, and with the wood that he had cut for the burnt offering, set out for the place of which God had told him.
>
> On the third day Abraham got sight of the place from afar. Then he said to his servants: 'Both of you stay here with the donkey, while the boy and I go up yonder. We will worship and then come back to you.' Thereupon Abraham took the wood for the burnt offering and laid it on his son Isaac's shoulders while he himself carried the fire and the knife. As the two walked on together, Isaac spoke to his father Abraham. 'Father,' he said. 'Yes, son,' he replied. Isaac continued, 'Here are the fire and the wood, but where is the sheep for the burnt offering?' 'Son,' Abraham answered, 'God himself will provide the sheep for the burnt offering.' Then the two continued going forward.
>
> When they came to the place of which God had told him, Abraham built an altar there and arranged the wood on it. Next he tied up his son Isaac, and put him on top of the wood on the altar. Then he reached out and took the knife to slaughter his son. But the Lord's messenger called to him from heaven, 'Abraham, Abraham!' 'Yes, Lord,' he answered. 'Do not do the least thing to him. I know now

> how devoted you are to God, since you did not withhold from me your own beloved son.' (Genesis 22:1–12)

This story reveals several strands about the nature of sacrifice as it is engendered into the psyches of men. Three aspects are of particular relevance: (a) fathers preparing their sons for sacrifice, (b) sacrifice to ideals and (c) rejecting feelings.

(a) Fathers preparing sons for sacrifice

The consistent theme of history is one of sons being prepared for sacrifice. They are trained for warfare, and valued for their prowess in overcoming the pain of their flesh to make their fathers proud. Those who stay too close to mother are derided and rejected. Those who strive to become champions win the fair maiden. Ask most men who have sons if they have different expectations of them than daughters. Of course they have. Scratch beneath the surface of male thinking and you get primal feelings of passion for the boy who can push himself beyond the limit. Tom Wolfe's novel *The Right Stuff* portrays it so well and in calling it 'the right stuff' eloquently asserts the value that generations of men have been programmed to believe. The ability to push the outside of the envelope, to go beyond the comfort zones, to risk all is the right stuff of manhood.

This way of cultivating and directing male energy has resulted in great benefits in the evolution of the human family. Enormous development in technology and communications, brilliant advances in science and medicine. The possibilities for global food resources and solutions to life-threatening poverty and disease. The dark side reveals cruelties on a scale hardly imaginable to a sensitive mind. Violence and addiction, widespread fatherlessness, a contempt for the beauty of the environment, and a loss of interest in the sacred, are legacies we may not survive long enough to learn from. In this century alone men have killed and maimed tens of millions of their fellow human beings. And most have been slaughtered in the developed, educated, wealthier and sophisticated societies. If the world were ruled by women it would have a different shape and form. It would have different strengths and weaknesses, perhaps we would be spending more on saving the planet and its people and less on discovering the geology of Mars. Such a speculation is interesting but perhaps futile in terms of the immediate future of Western societies in particular.

It is somehow fashionable to deride men who respond to these powerful forces as simply boys being boys. And yet we no longer swing from trees, we no longer live in fear of many deadly diseases and marauding animals, we no longer live in a small world confined internally by ignorance and externally by inability to travel or communicate. So much of what we now take for granted in terms of our physical security, health and knowledge is here because many generations of men were prepared to push themselves beyond the comfort zones to win a prize, whether that prize was admiration, knowledge, power or whatever was granted to those who persevered towards the goal. But the price paid is enormous and many men who couldn't cut it were rejected and often marginalised; some lived in quiet despair, others lived out their anger in destructive and self-destructive lifestyles.

When Abraham went up the mountain to sacrifice his son he represents all those who considered the safety and well-being of their male child a lesser value than the cause in which they believed. The son's well-being is the province of motherhood, his pride and power in the world is the responsibility of fatherhood. Men are continuing to pay a sometimes fatal price for this influence.

(b) Sacrifice to ideals

Both the historical accounts and the literature of mythology also tell us that idealism is a powerful element in the nurturing of the male psyche. In general, the themes concern the fight for truth or the testing of one's courage. Abraham was prepared to sacrifice his son to prove his faith. (Ironically, I think he would have proved his faith better by saying no.) What is of particular relevance here is that his faith was in an ideal. God is the omnipotent male, the higher power, the centre of meaning and the holder of truth. He tests Abraham's loyalty by asking him to sacrifice his beloved son. In order for Abraham to prove his faith he must detach from all that is humane. The relationship between father and son is subordinate to the relationship between father and his belief. He must not allow his feelings for his son to determine the outcome. Rather he must leave aside the call of his feelings and rely on some other guide, that which is called faith.

Another symbolic ritual that encapsulates this tradition is that of circumcision. On a recent visit to a Middle Eastern country I saw many circumcision parades. The boys were usually about five years old. In general, the father proudly led the parade as other men played a variety of instruments in celebration of the coming event. The boy dressed in white and garlanded with flowers and decoration sat on a donkey or in some cases a donkey and trap. I shuddered as I watched one of the parades, I could physically feel empathy with these young boys as they faced into what for me is the mutilation of their penis. I was in the company of a local man whom I had grown to like and respect. He was well educated, deeply aware of political and philosophical questions, and had a deep insight into cultural differences. He challenged me on my reaction telling me that these young boys would feel a little discomfort and would be playing at the circumcision party later in the day. His comments did little to allay my sadness at what for me now is a ritual embedded in culture that begins the process of preparing boys for sacrifice. And in the Jewish tradition this is exactly its meaning. God told the Israelites that they would circumcise all male children as a mark that they were his people. This means that they belong to God. Both the story of Isaac and the ritual of circumcision mean that men are there for the purpose of some calling or vocation that will not take their suffering into account.

On my return from the holiday I looked closely at photographs of these events and I don't think I'm imagining that these boys were afraid, but trying to be brave. I think about how their fathers could be so proud for their little boys. And of course they were proud, walking tall and striding forth, announcing to the world the depth of their happiness for their young sons. What did each have to let go in order to forget his son's fear and pain and encourage him and affirm him to take the pain in his stride, to become like his father who also once rode on a donkey into this place of the beginning of manhood. Fathers must detach from their own fear, their own memory in order to celebrate the event. Detachment then is a central requirement for a righteous man and by implication of true masculinity. Men must leave the realm of their feelings, their hopes, their needs and their loved ones once they have been called to a higher purpose. Each generation has some variation of the causes worth suffering and dying for. History reveals that many of them were, in reality, a farce.

Perhaps no area of life reflects this as clearly as the military. Young men are called on to offer themselves up for God and country. They must be convinced that the cause is worth expending their lives for. The people who do the convincing are also men who believe that they themselves have reached the wonderful heights of masculinity, a complete detachment from feelings and a total belief in the glory of an honourable death under fire. Stanley Kubrick's excellent film *Full Metal Jacket* illustrates this so well. The role of boot camp is to so damage the more sensitive feelings of young men that they will be able to become killing machines unhindered by compassion for those they will kill. The character of Private Pyle is used as a pinion to drive this point home. Dull and physically awkward, he is unable to surmount the challenge of the training. He is victimised and consistently ridiculed and degraded. One young man is given the responsibility of helping him, and takes on the task with sincerity and resolute determination. We see a relationship based on compassion emerging and eventually the dull and unacceptable soldier in the making begins to respond.

His progress is, however, inconsistent and eventually he makes a mistake by hiding food in his locker. This offence is seen as a failure of masculinity (needing to comfort himself or satisfy his hunger) and he is punished. This time, though, the very able and quite cruel sergeant does what is often seen in the history of masculine warrior training, he makes the group responsible for the failures of the individual. From then on every time Private Pyle fails the test of warrior masculinity, his colleagues are punished. An extraordinary scene then occurs where one night, after he causes them trouble again, they tie him down and each member of the platoon takes a turn at hitting him. In a dramatic conclusion his mentor, and symbolic father, stands and waits struggling between his compassion for this unfortunate failure of a man, and the rite of passage of conforming to the demands of the group, and here is the important denouement: he beats him harder than any of the others. He has thus successfully beaten his own vulnerability, symbolised by the pathetic and wounded nature of his brother in arms. Eventually, Private Pyle kills himself and his buddies go to war. The film ends when after a bloody encounter the peaceable young man who entered boot camp and wanted to become a writer shoots the seriously wounded female sniper, and they 'haul ass' back to base as a team of blooded warriors, illuminated by fire, smoke and blood. The last line of the film is a fitting summary of the *raison d'être* for all the dehumanising of these young men: 'Yes, we were in a world of shit, but we were alive, and we were not afraid.'

He has learned to sacrifice himself and his personality to the call of his country. He has also followed the true path and has engaged in the role of father to the dead private. He sacrificed him rather than protected him. And in so doing he joined the ranks of the men who despise those who are unable to leave behind their needs and wants when the call to arms is made. To follow the ideal, be it to be brave, to kill the 'commies' or the 'gooks', to uphold democracy, to honour Allah, to destroy the infidel, or to follow whatever cause one engages in requires the sacrifice of oneself in some shape or other, and requires that one win regardless of the cost. This has been a part of the conditioning of men for generations. And some never recover.

(c) Rejecting feelings

Another aspect inherent in teaching men to sacrifice themselves to the ideal is that they must reject the real. The ideal relationship, namely Abraham's loyalty to God, is supreme over the real relationship with his flesh and blood son. Men are taught to live inside their heads, to look for the ideal, to miss the flesh and blood experiences of the present for some more faraway, less attainable possibilities. Thus, ideals become predominant in men's thinking and faith is supreme over feelings. When we combine these forces in terms of how we define men we see that they are taught to be detached from their feelings and attached to ideals. This allows them to move more freely into the frame of sacrificing themselves and others. This detachment is a two-edged sword. Once you learn to detach from feelings such as fear, vulnerability and sadness you also become detached from compassion, pity, sensitivity. It is then much easier to cause others to suffer.

When people complain that men are out of touch with their feelings they really mean that men are in fact focused on something else. There is a famous experiment in perception called the figure ground experiment that can help us clarify this matter. A figure is presented to the onlooker. It can be seen as a haggard old woman or a beautiful young lady. The key element in perception is that the figure cannot be seen as both at the same time. Similarly, when men are raised and conditioned to commit themselves to ideals and are required to cut away the call of their feelings then they cannot at the same time be expected to remain connected to their emotional selves.

Emotional detachment and a focus on ideals has given men the power to dominate the natural world, to break through barriers in knowledge and to create and build the modern world. I can sit here in a comfortable room, listen to gentle music in the background, type my ideas on a word processor, and phone a friend if I get bored or restless, because certain men spent their lives working on pioneering these developments. In spending their energies in this way many became distant from those around them, were not particularly loving spouses or caring fathers, and often left a legacy of heartache in their wake.

(ii) Men are raised to protect and provide for women

For the vast majority of men their first experience of womankind is their relationship with their mother. Their direct experiences in the relationship are gradually replaced in influence by their observation of how their father relates to the mother, and then as childhood progresses the broader picture of the social treatment of women comes into play. For most of human history there are significant themes in each of these areas that play a crucial role in male development.

One of the central planks of the revolution that has occurred in the battle for social equality for women has been the issue of male domination. Historically, male domination has been expressed through ownership and possession. It is part of the human story that many tribes and societies which gained power or domination over others considered that the ownership of human beings through slavery was a realistic and useful part of their ability to function. Some of the great civilisations, ones which are the foundation for so much of our modern society — those of the Greeks, the Egyptian and Roman cultures — would never have succeeded without the use of slave labour. Slavery continues today in certain countries. In one African country the price of a slave is roughly £30 depending on their physical condition. While no one who has developed a high view of human life can condone the practice, it is important to recognise its role in our history. The ownership of people is not in itself a feminist issue. It was part of the developmental history of many human societies.

It seems a realistic generalisation that human beings from whatever epoch of history protect what they own. Men protected women in general because they believed that they owned them. The traditional picture of men being responsible for protecting and providing for women gradually emerged from the social reality that men considered women as part of their property. The whole issue of dowries being agreed as part of a business deal is a clear symbol of the transfer of assets. Polygamy was an intrinsic part of many cultures where the number of wives a man had was a symbol of his wealth and respectability and position in the community. Other cultures are prepared to kill their womenfolk if they lose their virginity before marriage, or refuse an arranged marriage; some still hold this practice. In one Middle Eastern country today, one quarter of the homicides are what are called honour killings, whereby brothers and fathers kill their sisters or daughters if they consider that they have brought shame on the family. Obviously, these people consider that their womenfolk are their property and that they have no right to choose who to be loved by or to have a relationship with. And so, just as men are the property of God, or some ideology adhered to by the society, women are the property of men.

I had a very informative and heated encounter with a woman on the issue of woman as property many years ago when I lacked the wisdom to realise just how hurt and angry some women are on behalf of the downtrodden and misused members of their gender. We were discussing the rite of marriage and in particular the part where the father of the bride walks up the aisle and 'gives her away'. I suggested that this was a meaningful part of the ceremony and would feel it something that I would like to take part in if my own daughter marries. I view this part of the marriage rite as a symbol of letting go the father–daughter emotional bond as she leaves the most significant male in her life for a new relationship, that with a spouse or partner. To ritualise this passage, like so many centrally important passages in life, including birth, death and adolescence, is a way of helping to name it and to process the emotional consequences for all concerned. As I attempted to present my views I soon realised that I was heading for the rocks on a turbulent sea. I tried without success to explain my thinking. In her mind this rite was an archaic expression of the man who owned his daughter giving her away into the possession of another man, and the whole dastardly act stank of arrogance, misogyny and plain primitive ignorance! She noted her disappointment in me as someone she thought had grown beyond such narrow and chauvinistic attitudes. I terminated the conversation as soon as was feasible and took my by now rather battered ego away for further reflection. I can see that for some the issue of woman as male property is still tied into this kind of ritual, and that consequently they may feel it to be demeaning and unnecessary.

Men saw their women as belonging to them, and thus they protected them from other men, from marauding enemies and from wild animals. They were seen as repositories for a man's children, incubating his seed (it is only since the nineteenth century that it became widely known that females produced eggs) and providing him with children. A large family and a great number of sons were marks of success and achievement. It is true to say that a bigger family usually brought protection in old age and more sons made it possible to increase one's power in the clan or tribe. Men did not necessarily treat 'their' women well or protect them from abusive treatment on their own part. There were some exceptions to these trends, societies that emerged where women were predominant, but, in general, the history of the human family is a story of men believing that they owned women.

Gradually, in those cultures that continued to evolve towards pluralism, those that developed intellectually, the Greeks and

Romans for example, the notion of woman as property began to weaken. In later times, as democracy emerged as a feasible and workable type of social arrangement, it became possible for women to throw off the shackles of oppression that dominated their lives throughout the ages. Much remains to be achieved in this regard. The vestiges remain in the protective aspects of men's role towards women. Protecting women became a valued element in masculinity and was idealised and romanticised in story and fable. Greek mythology is strewn with the heroics of men saving women. Perseus, after killing the Medusa, travels to the East and discovers the fair maiden Andromeda, chained to a rock to be offered to the sea monster to allay its anger. Made invincible by the talismans and the spell of Medusa's head, he slaughters the monster and saves the fair Andromeda. The knights of the round table seemed to spend much of their time, when not searching for the grail, protecting women. Sirs Gawain, Galahad and Lancelot are representative of knightly endeavours in the age of chivalry. Robin Hood rescued Maid Marian from the evil clutches of the sheriff of Nottingham. More recently, the enormously successful film *Titanic* has, at its core, a love story that features the rescue of a woman, initially from an unsuitable man and eventually from death. Leonardo DiCaprio surrenders his place on the raft and dies so she can have some hope for survival. In his sacrifice he represents all those men who, in historical reality, let the women and children go first as they awaited their doom.

This kind of conditioning runs very deep and is not simply the stuff of story and fictional drama. I remember the awful day in the summer of 1998 when the terrorist atrocity in Omagh took the lives of twenty-nine people. After the optimism felt by most that, at last, some peace was achievable in the North of Ireland, it was like a sucker punch to those who care about such things. The news coverage was extensive and the scenes of devastation were harrowing. One particular feature I remember well was becoming tearful when one newscaster specified that a certain number of women and children were killed. I reflected on this deep feeling that hit me and realised that I was not as moved by the fact that men were killed. I believe that most people have the same kind of reaction and this in the present context bears thinking about. Why do we consider it more tragic when women and children die violently than when men die? What is it in our psychology that tells us that a man's life is not as important as that of a woman or a child? There is something wrong here, and it is endemic. Had children not been killed I believe we would still react differently to the death of women than to that of men. These reactions, I believe, are based on centuries of cultural conditioning. It is inherent in the literature that underpins modern society that men have some responsibility towards women that women do not have towards men.

Implicit in this deeply held bias is the notion that women need protection, and that it is a virtue in a man if he offers this. The age of chivalry gave particular attention to this phenomenon. Men walk on the outside when in public. Why? Tradition has it that when people threw the contents of their chamber pots into the streets it was more likely to hit the person walking on the outside. St Paul gave spiritual guidance on the matter ensuring that this attitude towards woman was enshrined into the tenets of Christianity, the religion that has shaped most of the structures and institutions in modern Western culture. His teaching positions the woman as 'the weaker vessel' — God is the head of the man and the man is the head of the woman.

The most up-to-date research suggests that there is no biological basis for these beliefs. Yes, men are physically stronger in terms of raw power, women are stronger in terms of endurance. The female brain is smaller but more densely packed with neurons. Without the benefit of this information, and because of cultural bias, between folklore and religion we have guaranteed that a boy child born into most cultures will grow up in traditions that ask him to protect women. The consequence of this is that he also picks up the message that women are in some way weaker.

In our own culture and that of most of Western Europe and the United States, from their earliest years young boys have read the stories, watched the television programmes or heard the accounts of men rescuing women. They usually do this by risking life and limb to do battle with a monster or dragon, or by simply killing a bad man. Bad men are those who get drunk and shoot people or steal cattle or rob banks. Really bad men are those who hurt women or children. Heroes are good men who risk their lives and sometimes give their lives to kill or capture the bad men, wonderful heroes are those who save the human family by rescuing the women and children.

The modern man can no longer go to the frontier and shoot the marauding bears, carve a homestead out of the scrub and clear the land and raise crops. Now he does his providing and protecting by making money, by getting promoted, by being better than other men at any number of activities, so that he can be admired as being successful by those he loves. Those who cannot achieve in this way become angry, and some will vent their anger on the only one who stays around long enough to become the target, their wife or partner. Others turn their anger inward and become depressed and despairing. Those who stay on the merry-go-round of achievement and success become stressed and sick, with short fuses, easily triggered and swift to react with impatience and anger.

Deep down, men sense that the world has changed and that man as hero/rescuer is no longer desirable. And thus the deepest conditioning about men's role in relationship to women is redundant. He is lost, but here's the irony, he cannot admit it. Consequently, he cannot make the changes needed, for to admit his sense of fear and confusion is to break with the deepest teachings, often instilled when he was just a little boy by the one he wanted to be so proud of him, the other woman, his mother. To make the changes that are needed to become healthy in the modern world he risks the greatest of all betrayals: he must break the tie with mother, a tie of profound power, and one of which the vast majority of men have no conscious awareness. We will examine this issue in a later chapter.

A modern example of the effects of this kind of cultural conditioning is found in a recent film, *Falling Down*. The central character played by Michael Douglas is a middle-class professional man who is in the process of psychological disintegration. He battles through the urban jungle trying to 'come home' to his wife and child. There is a protection order out against him and we only get the hints that he was hostile towards his wife, and that his relationship with his mother was a sick one. The film is a story of loss. His loss of dignity, his pride and his need for connection are all explored. The film ends when he is confronted by a policeman who tells him that he knows he was going to kill his wife and child and then kill himself. There is now no way back. His last words to the policeman are that he is going to pull a gun on him because if he is shot by the cop his life insurance will be there for his family. He dies of a gunshot wound to the heart after pulling a plastic water pistol from his pocket.

The psychology of this story is reflective of what happens to a man who is conditioned to behave and believe in ways that have become redundant. The character in the film no longer has any value, he has lost everything and has nothing else to believe in. He wants to possess his wife and child and in his disordered thinking the only way he can do so is to bring them with him in death. As the film reaches its climax the central character realises that, after all, his life can have meaning by way of his death. His death becomes meaningful to him when he realises that he can use it to provide the wherewithal for his wife and child to become financially secure. Here we see the two aspects of men's conditioning coming into play — sacrifice yourself and provide and protect.

Counsellors and therapists see that this form of thinking is not simply Hollywood exaggeration. Insurance companies know well that many more men would kill themselves if suicide did not negate life insurance policies. One example, in my own experience, poignantly reflects this issue. Jack was a colleague of a good friend of mine, who told me his story after his death.

Jack, a businessman in his late forties, having experienced much financial difficulty and the failure of one business, saw his new business slowly crumbling. He found a life insurance company that had a clause in its life policy that meant it would pay out even in the case of suicide as long as the suicide occurred at least thirteen months after the policy was instigated. Jack was hard-working, middle-class, with a very strong belief in the traditional role of men providing for their families. Facing financial ruin, he had a choice between sacrificing his life and providing for his family on the one hand, or holding on to his life and living in relative poverty, with all its implicit failure and shame, on the other. No college fees for his up-and-coming teenage children, no second car for his wife, no more respect from colleagues all beckoned for his future.

One week after the thirteen months were up Jack killed himself. His death was not the impulsive act of a mentally disturbed person. Rather, from his point of view, it was a rational, calculated decision, made more than a year in advance, a successful outcome to solve a problem that could not be solved any other way. The men I have talked to about this event have quite a level of understanding and empathy for Jack's situation. Quite a few of them, in fact, think just like him. After his funeral the consensus among many of his colleagues (for the most part self-made businessmen and hard-driving professionals) was that he had done the decent thing.

The conditioning of men as protectors leave many with very confused ideas and feelings about women. Most men will acknowledge that they are attracted to them sexually, desire their love and affection, are intrigued, puzzled and sometimes fearful of them. Some men react to the expectations to protect by becoming disdainful and angry with women. In general, men have a deeply held belief that the best they can do for women is to protect them and provide for them. What else can they offer? Men are told that they are not particularly good at communicating feelings, especially those that involve sensitivity or vulnerability. They are not particularly good at listening because they get impatient with detail and want to find a practical and hopefully quick solution. Men are often frustrated that things of the heart are so complicated. Many feel incompetent and insecure in relation to women, but have been very firmly taught that they have no right to such confusion and that they better hide it beneath a veneer of confidence. So men often come up with silly solutions to complex relationship problems, or simply ignore them and hope they will go away. Turning their attention to the areas in which they feel competent and playing to their strengths, they operate out of the programme that was so clearly taught to them throughout childhood: be brave, be strong, compete and achieve.

Male loneliness and vulnerability remains an uncharted territory, with its own secret architecture, often unavailable to the ministration of those who love them. Men become alienated and resistant and the women who love them find no landing place for their hearts' concerns. Much of this is a legacy of making men into protectors. There are serious consequences for this in terms of men's abilities to relate to women as equals, or in some cases to relate to them at all. We will examine these issues more fully in later chapters.

(iii) Men are defined by what they achieve

A third theme that emerges when we examine the influences that go to shape men is that of defining men by what they achieve. There is a scene of extraordinary power in the film *The Field* (based on John B. Keane's play) that poetically expresses how men are taught to define themselves in this way. The Bull McCabe, a powerful, hardened and passionate man, is trying to explain to the priest why he should encourage the American businessman not to outbid him in buying the field. He tells him a story of his youth. When he was a young boy he worked in the field with his mother and father saving the hay. His mother tied the stooks as his father cut and he carried. His mother had been ailing in health and on this day she died in the field as she worked. They laid her comfortably on the grass and his father asked about getting the priest for her (an absolute condition of the care of the dying in the culture of the time). His young son looked at rain clouds gathering and asked his father if they should finish the hay first. When he looked to his father for a response he saw tears of pride in his eyes. His father was moved deeply that his son now understood his life task and had captured the meaning of his role as a man. He must love the field and in turn build on his father's achievement of making it productive and well cared for, thus making it the pride of the community. This young man's priorities are clear and he would make a good heir. Richard Harris plays this part with such conviction and power that it seems to me quite probable that, like many men of his age, he himself understood the meaning inherent in this scene.

Another aspect of this issue becomes evident when we see what happens to men when their sense of achievement is removed. In the early part of my career I worked for a training organisation that provided adult retraining for people who had lost their jobs. One particularly harrowing type of course was called 'Building on Experience'. The participants were mostly men in their late forties and early fifties who had become redundant during the massive economic recession of the 1980s. Many had left school in their teenage years to work on the land. As they reached early adulthood many travelled to England to work on construction sites. They made money to send home to their families, many of whom were poor. All they needed was a strong body and a willingness to suffer. After a period of two or three decades when the economy recovered they returned home, settled down and worked in factories that grew up as part of the economic booms of the 1960s and 1970s. When the recession hit they were made redundant in their droves.

Many ended up on state-sponsored training programmes that were little more than a rather cynical exercise in accounting. Training programmes were funded by the European exchequer whereas welfare payments were funded by state finances. There was a strong incentive in government to place these men on training programmes and thus save the exchequer the cost of their welfare payments. In many cases the programmes had little or nothing of substance to offer these men. The insult of treating them like children was added to the injury of lost dignity. In any case I met them at the premature end of their working lives while I, young enough to be one of their sons, was in the early stage of mine. I learned far more from them than they did from me.

One of the saddest experiences in my working life was to witness the futility and despair these men felt about themselves simply because they had no jobs. What struck me forcibly at the time was that, for many, the jobs they had lost were menial and often very boring and sometimes dangerous. They could not be missing the work itself, what they were missing was the value that society had placed in having a job, any job. They had internalised this expectation which said that they were now lesser men, failures and worthless. It would have been an extremely useful training course to help such men change their image of themselves rather than exacerbate their pain by training them in interview skills, doing CVs, writing letters and so on for jobs they knew they would not get. As one very articulate and intelligent man, a participant on the course, described it, 'I'm fifty-two years old and already consigned to the dustbin, to be supported by social welfare for the rest of my days.' He died from a heart attack two years later.

My memory of these men came back to me recently as I watched *The Full Monty*. Most people consider this film hilarious and while I had my share of laughs at it, its success as a comedy intrigues me somewhat. The story of the film is simple.

The characters are unemployed men from a blue-collar industrial area in England. The main character is a young man who is separated from his wife, who because of losing his job cannot afford to provide child payments, or fund his son's school tour, and is thus deeply distressed at losing his son's respect, especially now as his ex-wife has a new man in her life, one who has a good job and can provide for her. Another key character is the former plant manager who continues to wear his shirt, tie and jacket to the unemployment centre because he has not yet told his wife that he has no job. He persists in sending letters of application to companies much to the derision of the rest who tease him about his desperation. He shows them a file full of rejection notices. He is terrified at how his wife will react when she finds out that there will be no holiday this year, and that the house will probably have to be sold. A third character has become impotent, his sexual dysfunction resulting from a combination of depression and low self-esteem. He grows to despise his worsening weight problem as he comfort-eats to cope with his distress.

All this provides a great context for black comedy. These and other marginalised characters set out to imitate the well-known Chippendales male stripper group as a way of trying to make some money and solve the financial problems for those who still depend on them. There is something funny about these utterly unsuited characters trying to carry this off. Without seeming too prosaic, however, I was left wondering, when the laughter died down, if a film like this was made about women taking off their clothes to make money for their dependants, would people have found it so amusing.

It was difficult for me to suspend disbelief sufficiently to enjoy the film. The characters reflected so accurately the sadness and despair that I saw in many of the men I worked with and described above. Yes, they laughed at their ordeal, especially when with each other. But their laughter was akin to whistling past the graveyard, a denial of fear and an attempt to hide their pain from each other. Many, I'm sure, kept their tears for the darkness and isolation of night. Men are destroyed when they lose their sense of being worth while, and they lose their sense of worth when they cannot achieve. This is the legacy of training men, generation after generation, to compete with each other and to be valued in the eyes of their community by their achievements.

Summary

In this chapter I have examined, albeit briefly, three elemental forces in the shaping of men. These forces are part of the social construction that defines men's role in the world and has evolved gradually throughout our history. The structure of our modern world is largely influenced by the effects of these in producing men who are idealists, protectors and achievers. These are the men we uphold as successful, worthy of respect and honour. In the next chapter I will examine more closely how these influences are trained into men from the beginning of childhood throughout education and into adulthood.

3 The Ties that Bind

Introduction

In the previous chapter I argued that men have been subject to certain influences that programme their lives and sense of identity. These influences have been part of the human story for millennia. They were accepted as an intrinsic part of reality rather than as an important but changeable set of socially accepted norms and beliefs. They lie underground in the psyches of men, whose ways of being in the world are driven, often unconsciously, by them. Many of the serious problems that regularly feature in the lives of men are direct consequences of men trying to shape themselves in response to these subtle but powerful inner voices. In this chapter I will examine how boys are treated by those responsible for their upbringing, so that they will develop the traits and characteristics considered desirable for masculinity. The primary influences are those of parents and school. It begins, as always, with mothers and fathers.

Mothers and sons

Every mother-son relationship is unique. And yet if we are to try to make some sense of what makes men the way they are we must look at some elements of their earliest relationship and perhaps get some vague outlines of the general principles that are at work. In what ways do mothers pass on the three influences outlined above to their sons? How do they encourage boys to sacrifice themselves, how do they communicate that boys should protect women, and how do they encourage boys to define themselves by their achievement? Much of the research on child rearing has focused on the way parents 'socialise' children. In other words, how do parents teach their children to become part of the social world? And consequently, how do children learn to identify themselves as male or female?

Some research suggests that even from the first moments of life, little boys are seen by parents as being more alert and independent and by implication as having fewer emotional needs than infant girls. Ironically, when little boys themselves are studied it appears that they are in fact more needy, cry for longer periods on average, and experience higher anxiety levels faster when left alone. In general, however, in the early part of infancy and early childhood the bond between mother and son is based on nurturing care. The model of manhood that every mother has within her is not influential in these early stages. Her role, unless she is disordered or damaged in some fundamental way, is not dependent on the gender of the child. She fondly nourishes and cherishes the infant. Gradually, however, as childhood progresses some subtle changes begin to take effect. Her picture of what it means to be a boy influences her interpretation of his reactions. He is let away with being troublesome more easily than a girl child. She smiles at his antics when he is pushing the boundaries, and thereby reinforces his assertiveness. She reacts more slowly to him when he cries and thus begins training him in a lesson that generally lasts throughout boyhood — that vulnerability is not allowed. He must therefore repress and control his feelings.

Perhaps the greatest wound one can inflict on any human being is to punish them for their feelings so that these feelings disappear. This is because feelings are essential to experiencing oneself as a human being. Once the capacity to feel is gone then the person as a unique identity is lost. That men have consistently and resolutely been trained to repress, suppress and deny their feelings is a grave and serious injustice to their humanity. It is also at the heart of many of the horrors that have bedevilled mankind. Let us look a bit more closely at how one's feelings develop and what happens when they are injured.

Feelings are experiences that occur in the internal world of a person. They begin in the womb in their simplest form, as sensual reactions of pleasure or pain. During infancy these sensual reactions become more differentiated from simple pain/pleasure experiences to a more complex spectrum involving joy, sadness, anger, love. They also become attached to events in the infant's and child's life. Thus, feelings of pleasure, warmth, comfort and joy become associated with being fed, soothed and caressed by a loving mother; conversely, feelings of anger and sadness become associated with hunger, being left alone or being neglected. As the child develops, they build a store of emotional experiences into their psychological identity. And importantly they build a relationship with these feelings. It is this relationship that is targeted by parents and society in shaping the boy who will become a man. In general, the boy is taught in a myriad of ways to reject certain feelings, and to embrace and cultivate others. Mothers begin this process during early childhood and as we shall see this is exacerbated by fathers and later in school.

The part that childhood experiences play in weakening girls and reinforcing their position as less important than males is well documented in the works of feminist writers. What is less clear is the impact on little boys when they observe the different treatment being meted out. They learn that little girls are in need of more care, of gentler treatment, that they are less robust and should be loved whether or not they have done something to deserve it. Little girls should be loved and cared for by virtue of being little girls, little boys on the other hand should be loved because they are able to do stuff. This is a central element in the different ways that boys are treated in their developmental years. Mothers are part of this process and in doing this prepare young men to be protective towards women.

As they grow through childhood mothers express pride in their achievements. They are not expected to relate to their mothers to the same extent as a daughter. Mothers as well as responding more slowly to little boys' distress also speak less to them. They are more likely to make vocalisations to little girls and spend more time doing so. As the child becomes more adept with language the communication between mothers and daughters takes a different slant to that of mothers and sons. Research shows that when dealing with a difficulty mothers spend longer talking with their daughters, and most importantly are more likely to discuss the emotional aspects, such as how the little girl feels about something and how the mother herself feels. When discussing similar issues with little boys the mothers talk less and focus the communication on what the little boys do. The emphasis is on behaviour rather than feelings. Conversations with mother during childhood are a key element in learning communication skills and in building a communication bridge with others in later life. Small wonder then that little girls, who are neurologically better equipped for language to begin with, develop better communication skills very early on. Little boys are directed towards a more silent, less verbal and more problem solving life from the very beginning.

Neither are little boys expected to help out with the household chores to the same extent. In this incubation period little boys are being cultivated to see achievement as more important than relationships. The influence at work here is the historical reality that women were affirmed and recognised for bearing children. Their sense of value, identity and achievement were and to a lesser extent still are lived out in the lives of their children, particularly the success and achievement of their sons. American sociologist and feminist author Nancy Chodorov argues effectively that as long as mothers live through their children they will continue producing men that need to prove themselves. Furthermore, it is her conclusion that 'women's mothering generated, more or less universally, a defensive masculine identity in men and a compensatory psychology and ideology of masculine superiority. This psychology and ideology sustained male dominance.'

Mother-son relationships begin a shaping of men towards a particular direction, a suppression of vulnerability, a focus on achievement, and a lessening of communication skills. In the modern world all of these trends are in place before the little boy goes to school. When he gets there these subtle and not so subtle influences are taken a step further and integrated into his educational experiences.

Fathers and sons

The elements of child rearing described above are in general also a feature of fathers' relationships with sons. In addition to neglecting boys' vulnerability, prizing them for achievement, and treating girls more gently, fathers bring some additional elements into play in preparing boys for manhood. One of these is ensuring that boys become distant from mothers. It seems a feature of most adult men that they worry if their son is seen to have too close a relationship with mother. The father of modern therapeutic psychology, Sigmund Freud, built a whole theory of personality on this issue. He believed that a boy falls in love with his mother and becomes terrified of his father's wrath lest he discover the little boy's lust for the mother, who is, after all, his first love object. The boy resolves this conflict (the famed Oedipus conflict) by drawing away from mother and identifying with the father. Failure to resolve this conflict led, in Freud's view, to all manner of adult neurosis. I believe that Freud developed this theory to explain a widespread phenomenon in child rearing, that of breaking the bond between mother and son so as to cultivate a more hardened and less sensitive emotional character. Freud's beliefs that this process is a necessary part of healthy male development, and that there is a sexual content involved, are, however, to my mind, suspect.

If we stay with the main argument of this book, namely that

men are created in order to fulfil the requirements of a particular society, then we can see how important it is that boys be separated from mother influence. Such influence is more likely to generate a 'softer' male, one who is interested and intrigued by relationships, who is more sensitive to feelings, perhaps more introverted and moved by interior forces, more concerned with giving and nourishing life. Males of this nature are less likely to fulfil the requirements of warfare, of acquisition, of invention and pioneering risk taking. And we must remember that all the great civilisations were based initially on success in warfare. When the requirements of warfare were no longer paramount it became possible for societies to live according to different priorities. As Warren Farrell nicely puts it, even the ferocious Vikings settled down into a peaceful existence when they were secure in their food source and in safety from their enemies.

Tearing boys away from mother influence is, in general, not a pretty sight. Most fathers do so with a certain degree of cruelty. This is because their efforts are often not a rational response based on concern for the boy, but rather a deep-seated primal reaction to a son who is seen as becoming effeminate, or weak. The ghosts of each man's own injuries around this issue lie dormant. Most men have been scarred through the toughening process of their own childhood and very few live in sufficient awareness of these as being an injury. Most in fact are proud of their scars. When their own child begins to cling too closely to the world of the female the old injury surfaces and action is taken. Words like 'pussy', 'wimp', 'spoiled' and 'mollycoddled' all spring to mind. The emotional reaction is generally a combination of contempt, anger and disdain tinged with anxiety. The strategy and tactics brought in to straighten the boy out include ridicule and rejection and up until recently, in many instances, physical violence.

John sits in my office and discusses his worry for his nine-year-old son. As his therapy unfolded John worked on his own problems of shame, anger, and distance in relationships. He is more aware and sensitive than a year earlier and deeply attached to his children. As he begins to discuss his son, a change appears in his demeanour. Gone is the furrowed brow, the sense of challenge to understand and in its place a look of disgust. He knows himself well enough at this stage to realise that the intensity of these reactions means that the difficulty is not his son but is within himself. John has a problem.

His son likes to play with a family of toy bears who have a little home in the woods and all the paraphernalia of a little bear family. He also likes to bake and to paint. John grew up in a world where such behaviour in a young boy would be scorned. He learned how to be a young man in the battlefield of sport. Injuries received were considered marks of valour and winning was the only reward. Losing was a matter of great shame and a spur for harder and tougher play next time. As a professional man in his late thirties he constructed his life around these virtues and his son's betrayal of all that is manly was making him sick. Had he not spent a year in search of some healing to many of the scars in his life, and had he lived at a different time, I have no doubt that John would have done what so many unaware and only half-evolved fathers do: he would have burned all his son's favourite toys and probably beaten him or continually ridiculed him, thus preparing another broken soul for the next generation.

Fathers also take on the task of moulding their son's attitudes to masculinity. They provide a working model of manhood which the boy child examines and tries to emulate. The message that many fathers give to sons is that life is not about relationships, it is about success, achievement and being brave. Many fathers are profoundly influential by virtue of their absence. Some are actually missing through divorce, separation or abandonment. The level of fatherlessness among families in the Western world is becoming an epidemic. Of those who are physically present many are emotionally absent. One statistic tells us that, on average, fathers spend less than fifteen minutes a day with their children.

This phenomenon of emotional distance in fathers is so widespread that many consider it an intrinsic element of masculinity. John Gray tells us that men must go into their cave when they return from work into the family. The boy who observes this is affected at two levels. He misses the nourishment of the relationship which would help him to communicate and to clarify the concerns in his own life with his father's listening ear. He also learns by example that men are silent and withdrawn.

Some fathers are, however, not withdrawn, some are in fact very present in a distressing and dysfunctional way. These are the men who return into the embrace of their family, hurt, worn out and angry at the toll that life is taking on them. These fathers can release much of the pent-up frustrations onto the people they feel safe to do so with and therefore reinforce the learning that the only emotions men are allowed to express are anger and aggression.

A principle at work here is that the quality of any human relation is a product of the qualities of the people in it. Fathers cannot cultivate a nourishing communicative and emotional relationship with sons if they themselves had these abilities scorned and broken during their own boyhood. Men cannot become emotionally present to their sons when they are not emotionally present to themselves. What fathers have done over the centuries is to teach their sons, through example, and through the way they treat them, to gird up their loins, to learn to suffer pain, to stay away from experiences that soften the heart, to fight, to be better than others, and to succeed. When sons cannot aspire to these lessons they develop a sense of failure that can haunt them for the rest of their lives.

Additionally, father's relationship with mother also tells the boy something of the nature of men and women. The boy observes his father and learns something of how to treat women. This can range from fathers who idealise their mates to those who scorn them. In general, the father will pass on some notion of the woman being different from the man whether that be positive or negative. Sons of fathers who abuse their spouses can become men who abuse their own mates, or conversely they develop an overly protective instinct towards mother. They become what John Bradshaw terms a 'surrogate husband' to their mother. In the latter case the boy grows up to see women as defenceless creatures in need of care and attention, often to the detriment of his own needs. He defines himself by virtue of being able to make his woman happy, and in so doing relives his past and symbolically rescues his mother. Fathers that idealise their mates inadvertently create a barrier for a young man to become proud of his masculinity. For ever after he is left with a feeling of being in debt if a woman loves him.

Schooling

The experience of school has a serious influence in confirming the messages instilled in a young boy. In my generation the messages were very clear. The modern experience of young people at school is less sexist and less damaging to their development. I spent several years in a boys-only boarding school in the mid-seventies. I have clear memories of the treatment of boys as being brutal both by those in authority and by the peer group. Competition ruled every aspect of life. The toughest fighter gained respect. Crying was scorned and ridiculed. The fastest runners, the best football players, the strongest athletes gained approval and licence. The majority of young boys could not feature as being the best at anything and had to settle for some scraps of approval here and there. In hindsight I can see that many of the boys and young men suffered a chronic low-level anguish each year there and I still marvel at the degree to which some of my peer group managed to survive the cruelties inflicted on them. Some of the priests who ran the place were also in trouble. Knowing what I know now I can see their unhappiness, their loneliness and their inability to cope with the complexity of young men growing up in a cold, emotionally neglectful and arid environment. From my conversations with others over the years I know that my experience was fairly typical of boys in that time and that in comparison to what happened the generation before we were relatively lucky.

Before the advent of modern education, which focuses almost exclusively on academic achievement, the task of teaching young men was essentially a matter of pitting them against each other so as to isolate and highlight their strengths and weaknesses. The goal was to hone and sharpen warriors. When you listen to those involved in sports training, which is the modern equivalent of warrior preparation, the topics most discussed involve the character traits exhibited by the young boys. Comments and questions such as does he have stamina? the killer instinct? does his head go down when he loses a point? is he able to 'put the game away' when ahead? all reflect these timeless influences of what young men should become. There is of course nothing wrong with this in terms of looking at the young person's strengths and helping them to learn about themselves, to learn teamwork, to learn endurance and so on. What is seriously wrong is that there is a definition of manhood at work that prizes some qualities and disdains others. This frame for masculinity is deeply entrenched, and it is, in my opinion, fundamentally unhealthy for young men in terms of growing up as balanced human beings.

That few men recognise their emotional injuries is a tribute to the effectiveness of the training. Young men are supposed to ignore their injuries. When we see a player running at the ball with broken fingers we admire his courage, we know that he would have been a brave warrior who would fight to the death to protect those he loves, or to pursue his beliefs and ideals. This is all very well and good at one level, but what does he do when the game is over? How can men so numb to their pain in one set of circumstances be expected to change roles and become sensitive and aware in another? Many men scorn this kind of talk.

They smile when they recall the brutalities inflicted on them, and summarise their experiences as having been good for them. They say, 'Look what happened to me, it didn't do me any harm,' 'It hardened me up for life,' 'Today's young people are too soft, they have no backbone.' These kinds of phrases are not simply denial, they come from a place of cauterised feelings. The men who say them have no experience other than that detached, logical and numbed place from which to experience life. The destruction of sensitivity, the crushing of feelings other than aggression and pride, the cultivation of a competitive approach to life that creates only winners and losers, with the winners in the minority, leaves most young men stranded when it comes to dealing with most of the more important issues in being an evolved and wise human being, loving oneself and others, the capacity for intimacy, parenthood, creativity and spirituality. Schooling completes the work already begun in the family and the boys that emerge as young men are for the most part emotionally injured as a result.

Summary

This chapter has examined some of the ways that boys are treated in their formative years so as to conform to the expectations and the moulds that are considered the making of a man. Mothers and fathers are particularly influential. Mothers nourish in the early days and then begin to train boys in the arts of neglecting their vulnerability, of proving their worth through achievement and in seeing girls as weaker and needing protection. Fathers also give these messages but additionally train boys, through the separation from the feminine, the black art of killing off their sensitivities, and of proving their worth through battle. In earlier times these battles were in real warfare, nowadays the battlefields are in sport, academic achievement, work and business. All of these influences are further reinforced through the process of schooling.

PART TWO

The Legacy: Damaged Men and Redundant Heroes

4 Dysfunctional Relationship to the Self

Introduction

We have seen in the previous chapter that certain kinds of child rearing practices are brought into play in raising men from boyhood, through adolescence, and on into manhood. They are developed in order to create the kinds of men that were needed for the evolution of society up to the present day. Like most complex aspects of human development there are positive and negative elements to these practices. And furthermore, what was once seen as a positive feature can become negative when circumstances change. A rather ironic example is that of the development of improved antenatal care for newborns and young children in Britain in the early part of this century. A significant element in this development was the complaint made by the military establishment that the physical quality of young British soldiers in the Boer War left much to be desired. By the implementation of improved health care the quality of young men improved significantly so that they were in much healthier condition when they were slaughtered in their tens of thousands in the killing fields of France during the First World War.

We will see in this section that many aspects of manhood that were cultivated as part of a different social reality are now causing grave problems for men. Although I have used the term dysfunctional to describe much of the legacy that is given to men I use the term in the limited sense that men are raised and taught to experience life in ways that are not helpful to their mental and emotional health. Many of these ways are in fact very functional for certain goals, such as dominating and defeating enemies, accumulating wealth and property, winning competitions, blind devotion to goals, idealism and endurance. Much of what is positive in modern-day society, the things we enjoy, that save us time and let us escape from menial tasks, that allow opportunity for personal growth, intellectual stimulation and development, are the benefits of men being cultivated in a particular way. In this section of the book we will look at the negative side of this issue.

The price of developing these traits in men is very high in terms of their own personal lives and in terms of the needs of today's society. In general, the damage that occurs to men as a result of these formative influences, in my opinion, can be seen in five central areas of personal functioning: (i) dysfunctional relationship to the self, (ii) isolation from other men, (iii) dysfunctional relationship to work, (iv) impoverished relationships with women, (v) inadequate skills for fatherhood. While these are all within the structure of the individual personality they have direct impact on the way that society functions. Men who have difficulties in these areas create great difficulties for other people. And in no small way they shape the general picture of what emerges in the whole of society. Not every man experiences difficulties in all these areas, and like most aspects of human function there is a range of effects. Some men will find themselves to be damaged in extreme ways in some or all of these areas, others find milder levels of difficulty in one or two, but very few men escape some level of destructive influences in at least one or two. This chapter examines the dysfunctional relationship with the self.

The concept of self is central to any discussion on human functioning. Every adult (with the exception of those who are seriously deranged) carries within them a sense of being a self, an individual in their own right. This self is built during the period of childhood and is profoundly influenced by the kind of treatment and guidance one receives from the primary caretakers, including parents, teachers and relatives. It consolidates during adolescence and is maintained throughout adulthood by way of certain fundamental experiences including the experiences of being in control, of being energetic (which simply means having energy), of being an agent of change, which means we can influence the direction of our lives and that we can make decisions and choices. These experiences might well be called experiences of the self in action.

Being a self also means knowing oneself as having certain abilities, strengths and weaknesses. It includes some perception of how one will be in the future (those who are in despair see a bleak future, those who are optimists see a positive one). It includes how one feels about certain things. These feelings can change over time, new likes and dislikes emerge, and the process of living can be a continuing experience of change. This might be called the basic structure of the self. The experience of being a self is therefore different to how one feels about it. Some people would like to have a different self, to be somebody else. Some don't like who they are, others are comfortable within themselves, and still others are positive and loving towards themselves.

We have now looked at two elements of the self: the sense of being an individual who is experiencing existence, and knowing something of the nature of that individual. Embedded in these two levels of knowing is a third aspect of self, the capacity to know, or observe oneself. Following Freud and Jung we can term this aspect the ego. A somewhat simplistic but perhaps useful analogy is to think of the ego as being akin to a driver in the car of the self. Both the driver and the car have certain qualities. Some cars are faster than others, some are bigger, brighter, older, and so on. The driver treats the car in certain ways, some are careful, others are risk-takers, some are respectful, others dismissive. The conscious ego has a similar relationship to the self. The main function of the ego is to protect and enhance the self. The male ego relates to the self through the prism of his beliefs about how to be a man. It chooses which qualities to develop and which to suppress, it reacts to situations, to love, to anger, to failure, to success in ways that enhance the self. The ego's relationship to the self is an internalisation of many of the influences of childhood.

Thus far then the self can be considered to have several aspects which comprise the unique constellation of feelings, thoughts and characteristics that goes to make up one's personality, and the ego which is aware of and relates to this constellation. As a direct result of the treatment of boys they develop into men who have particular problems in two areas of the self, a distortion of the ego and a damaged relationship to feelings. We will examine each separately.

(i) Distortion of the male ego

There are, in general, three kinds of difficulties that can emerge in the male ego. These are the inflated ego, the deflated ego and the emasculated ego. Let us look at each in turn.

The inflated ego

The inflated ego develops when a boy becoming a man is able to achieve the sense of pride and power being cultivated and encouraged by his environment. The masculine energy is channelled into the expansion of the ego and the ego's relationship to other aspects of the self is grounded in a sense of omnipotence and importance. All children go through a stage of narcissistic self-indulgence as a natural part of development. The memory of this stage of childhood is locked away. Over a number of years it is tempered through enough failure, disappointment and learning how to include others, to become a residue of infancy. During adolescence, however, a time when a young man struggles to find a sense of himself, these regressive infantile experiences can come back into experience. The heady feeling of being the best, the most important, is, for some, integrated into the now consolidating sense of self. It is also possible that the one who senses that he will never be good enough at whatever the particular currency of competition is at work during his formative years develops a sense of being above it, being too sophisticated, insightful or intelligent to engage in such trivial pursuit. He develops this grandiosity as a compensatory mechanism initially, but can in time begin to believe his own propaganda.

The inflated ego is reflected in a man who is in love with himself and yet knows little of the nature of love. His relationship to himself is based on an illusion that can last a lifetime. He is grandiose, proud and considers himself superior to others. One of the costs of the inflated ego is the failure of empathy. This has serious implications for the nature of his relationships. Empathy is the ability to see things from another's point of view and to experience the feelings that some one else experiences. The inflated ego is so self-absorbed that the feelings of others are of no relevance except in so far as they impact on him. When one is in a discussion with an inflated ego the conversation seems to consistently return to his concerns. He can be hell to work for unless people become part of his fantasy of being godlike. Those who stroke his ego, admire him and support his self-belief are given pride of place; those who reject him do not hurt him, they merely show themselves as having no taste.

Men whose egos are inflated are actually very easy to manipulate, and many find themselves at the top of corporate ladders. Equally, they can be found in the ranks of the criminal world. They become undone, however, when they experience failure, loss, the rebellion of their children, and old age. They have no natural skill to handle these limiting circumstances. They can react to these kinds of events by opening up to learning something or by developing some additional form of emotional sickness, most likely to be an addiction of some kind.

Peter has an inflated ego. He is available for therapy only

because he ended up in an addiction treatment centre for prescription drug abuse problems. His attendance at the treatment centre was forced upon him by combined threats from his family and his superiors at work. He attended, not out of any sense of belief that these people were right, but rather because he feared being shamed publicly more than anything else in life. After much confrontation from others in the treatment programme he began to reveal the extent of his pride and arrogance.

His work in the field of medicine gave him a profound sense of power. He was one of those who entered the field of medicine not out of a genuine compassion and calling to help others, but rather as a means of achieving the high level of social status that this kind of work received here, especially in the sixties and seventies. The money and prestige grew as he pursued more and more specialist training until he ultimately began to believe himself to be some sort of very special person; in everyday language he developed a Messiah complex. Those close to him on the other hand saw him as boorish, insensitive, and some laughed at him behind his back as he spoke in terms of his abilities and achievements. His patients found him cold and unsympathetic; those who paid him for private consultations were treated with a modicum of concern, those reliant on social health care were simply pieces of interesting research data.

His attendance at counselling was to try to repair his marriage, which was in the final stages of collapse. As a client he was very difficult to work with because his first instinct was to control the session, and to lecture me as to the nature of psychology. He had read some books on the topic and like many inflated egos was now an expert. Therapy lasted a brief time when it became clear that neither his wife nor I was going to be bullied into submission. He continues, albeit in a sober state, to ply his trade with his usual ebullience to this day.

I had a discussion recently with a female friend of mine about the intractable and difficult nature of the inflated ego. We talked about the nature of men who operate their lives from this place and she recounted an interesting event that seemed to me to reflect some elements of this disorder. She was at a social gathering which involved some of her peer group and some friends. One of the men at the event seemed to fulfil the picture of the inflated ego as I have described it. What was of particular interest was that his wife was a very perceptive woman. She had close friends and was quite sensitive and compassionate. Her friends wondered about how the relationship seemed to be thriving given their own reactions to this man. He was charming, successful and wealthy but very superior and self-confident and with little insight or depth. Few of them would say that they could really like him or seek in him the kind of intimacy and connection that most people want. In their conversation one of the group asked her how she managed her relationship and how she kept it so friendly and obviously relaxed. Her reply is a lesson worthy of a place in the politics of relationships. She said, 'I give him plenty of sex and treat him like a child.' Hearing this I was convinced that this woman understood the fundamental nature of the inflated ego.

She had compromised some of her own needs in order to have others fulfilled. She had financial security, a man that adored her while most likely not knowing her, and a good social life. The price she paid was a lack of emotional intimacy. Her winning formula with this man combined consistent affirmation of his rather simplistic notion of manhood, with protecting him from gaining any developmental insight into himself. The inflated ego is a retarded form of emotional life. It is but one of the consequences that can ensue from the emotional injuries inflicted on young boys as they are cultivated into men for the needs of society. A far more common disorder is that of the deflated ego.

The deflated ego

The deflated ego develops within a man when he believes himself to be inadequate to the tasks of manhood. The masculine energy is directed against the other aspects of the self. The man becomes his own enemy, and he internalises the rejection and contempt that inheres in the training of childhood. If the ego could be separated out into an external voice it would harangue, criticise and mock just as effectively as any hard-nosed football coach.

The core of the deflated ego is found in the role of competition that is a central part of masculine development. Every competition involves winners and losers. Winning is given as an essential trait of masculinity. To lose is to fail in one's task of being a man. The deflated ego develops in response to such failure. And for most men boyhood is replete with such failures. To miss the important goal, to feel too tired to continue the race, to fail the academic rat race, to be beaten in a fight with a peer, these and others represent the scars given to a young boy in his struggle to prove his worth as a young man.

Terrence Real exquisitely describes this process when he says:

> once we realise that the elusive 'masculine' does not exist inside the boy's psyche, but rather that it is a social construct to which the boy must bend and comply, we can understand why it is impossible for most boys to feel secure about it. Being 'man enough' isn't something one has definitively once and for all. It is something that is granted by the community of men whom we experience as watching, weighing and judging. To become a man — an act that is supposed to be quintessentially independent — in fact means that a male reference group consents to call one a man. The construction of manhood turns out to be as social as a sewing circle. Masculinity, unlike femininity, is conferred. And since it is bestowed, it can also be taken away.

In a similar vein, John Archer in his book *Male Violence* examines the way that masculinity is conferred through a consistent set of behaviours that are expected of young boys. He sees this as being a key issue in understanding why some men, particularly those in the impoverished classes, resort to violence. He argues that

> Perhaps the most important feature of it is that it is an achieved rather than an ascribed status. It arises from behaving in a particular way. During childhood, a boy can be ostracised because he does not, or cannot, reach acceptable standards of masculine behaviour; on the other hand, some girls may achieve honorary masculinity through being skilled at boys' games and activities. A boy's self-esteem is derived from taking part in a range of physical activities, and there is an emphasis on toughness for defining status. During adulthood, self-esteem is derived from a wider range of activities, notably occupational achievement. As we have seen in marginal suburban communities this source of status is generally not available.

The deflated ego reveals itself in many ways. Men who carry around a sense of shame for who they are may try to compensate by hard work, by silently withdrawing, by passive hostility, depression or chronic stress. The relationship with self is based on a sense of unworthiness. This, in turn, creates fear of being known. In the world of men it is important that vulnerability not be shown so that the true sense of self must be hidden behind some mask that can be seen to be successful in a certain way. The key here is the need to measure oneself in terms of the success being conferred by one's social context. The currency of such success has different coinage. For some their success may be in rebelling against the status quo. So many young men today get their sense of pride and self-worth from failing to conform to the expectations of society. What was once a rite of passage that young men went through in adolescence, namely mocking authority and cocking a snoop at the middle-class ethos, has for many become a way of life. The gang becomes a mini-society with its own rules and regulations, its own pecking order, where the toughest, the most brutal, the greatest risk-takers earn the spoils. For others, who stay in the mainstream, success may be measured by the size of the bank balance, the second car, the big house.

All of these efforts may mask a sense of unworthiness, a desperate attempt to prove oneself as a man. The key element here is that the perceived success is not truly integrated into the male self. He believes beneath his image that he has in some elusive way failed in some important task. Like the central character in Franz Kafka's *The Trial* he is waiting to find out the crime of which he has already been found guilty. It is interesting to examine Kafka's work from this perspective. It seems not a coincidence that 'Joseph K.', the accused, is a thirty-year-old banker. He has a position of authority and is treated with respect by those who work for him. This grim and bleak story is an account of the gradual realisation that all the positional power, flawed respect and social status will not protect this man from being accused and punished. Kafka himself was acknowledged to be a keenly sensitive man, a very passionate individual, intuitive, intelligent and easily hurt. His father on the other hand was a tough and rejecting figure, who was part of the wealthy merchant class and had no respect or value for Franz's love of writing. With no encouragement or support Kafka had to make a living by working as a clerk in an insurance company. This mundane office work had a terrible effect on him and perhaps led to his weakened physical condition, which resulted in his death at forty years of age. Deeply critical of his own work, towards the end of his life Kafka left strict instructions that all his writings, including notes, letters and unfinished work, be burned.

To some extent *The Trial* can be seen as autobiographical and reflects the anger Kafka felt at the loss of idealism and the compromising of the soul. This is the sin for which Joseph K. is being indicted. Many men sell out important parts of their lives for the sake of earning a living and earning some measure of respectability in the eyes of their peer group. Their relationship within the self carries within it a sense of having failed in some way. The inflated ego relies on and believes his image, the deflated ego strives to compensate for his sense of failure and weakness.

The emasculated ego

The key to understanding the emasculated ego is to examine the nature of masculine energy. We have seen above that in the inflated ego, the masculine energy is focused on expansion and grandiosity, in the deflated ego the energy is channelled into protection and defence. Both of these are dynamic in so far as the energy is creative. In the former it creates success and achievement in a bullish, dominant and sometimes cruel form at the cost of expression of a gentler and more relational character. In the latter it creates success and achievement in order to prove one's worth. In both cases the game of being a man is still being played according to the rules laid down in childhood, namely that the only true basis of manhood is success and achievement in some form of competition. The emasculated ego does not function by way of proving oneself. The masculine energy is denied and repressed. This is usually reflected in a passivity towards life. The ego has accepted defeat and no longer engages in life in any direct or challenging way. The person usually experiences a sense of ennui, of emptiness and boredom, there is no drive to expand personal boundaries of ability or relationship.

In considering the emasculated ego I remember reading another important philosopher that has greatly influenced Western thought. The emasculated ego looks like what Kierkegaard called living at the aesthetic level. According to Kierkegaard the least authentic form of human existence is the aesthetic stage. In this stage a person lives in the world of the senses and pleasure is the priority. His greatest challenge may be to cope with the rigours of indolence. It is a life that is devoid of true passion or commitment. From Kierkegaard's perspective many people surrender their idealism and settle for this kind of unaware and sensation-based existence. He believed that Western Europe in particular had fallen foul of a widespread acceptance of this condition. Much of his argument is taken up by later philosophers.

In the light of his anger at this form of living it is interesting to note that Kierkegaard was raised by an extremely strict and guilt-ridden father. A wealthy retired businessman, he was in Kierkegaard's words 'the most melancholy man I have ever known'. Kierkegaard's description of people living in the world of the senses, devoid of ideals and commitment, is partly based perhaps on his experience growing up with a father who was already broken by life.

For the emasculated ego the conditioning of childhood has so profoundly impacted on the young boy's development that he cannot identify sufficiently with the model of manhood being held up as an ideal. He is too frightened to fight, too hurt to be confident and too close to the feminine to risk losing it. He therefore retreats into the world of sensation. He may be artistic or a dreamer. Fantasy replaces reality as a focus of attention. Addiction to some form of mood-altering substance that creates a sense of communion and/or perceptual distortion such as hallucination becomes a great probability. There is no sense of doing battle with life. The male in this situation tends to regress into dependent relationships often repeating the childhood experience of passive dependence. The process of living is simply an urge to find a safe structure, cultivate pleasurable experiences, avoid competition and seek out nurturing care from a woman who is often, in essence, a surrogate mother. To borrow from Evelyn Bassoff's work in *Between Mothers and Sons*, she provides what she terms 'an evocative image of the absence of maleness' by drawing on the traditions of the Sambia tribe in New Guinea. According to their tradition a man depleted of male energy is a 'wasaatu': a mushy 'sweet potato' man who lacks resolve, self-discipline and commitment.

(ii) Damaged emotions

Thus far we have examined the effects of male conditioning on a man's sense of self. For the most part this is the cognitive aspect of his functioning. He thinks there is a certain way to be a successful man and behaves according to this inner guide. A second area where many men experience difficulty is in knowing their feelings, and being able to express them appropriately. One of the principal aspects of mental health is the ability to experience and express feelings. It is what makes us individuals and what separates us from robots or computers. Feelings affect everything about us, the way we relate to people, the experiences we have of our own happiness and fulfilment, the way we parent our children, the way we love our lovers. These and a lot more belong in the realm of feelings. If we are damaged in this part of our humanity we are at a great loss. We will see in this chapter that men as a group have been badly served in their development of this aspect of their lives. Damage to men's feelings tends to happen in two ways, detachment from feelings and inappropriate expressions of feelings.

The detachment from feelings

It is extraordinarily difficult to describe feelings to someone who is unaware of them. Let us imagine how we would describe the colour blue to a blind person. If we reflect for a moment on that problem we get some idea of the obstacles that some men face when confronted with the world of feelings. I encounter this reality regularly in working with men. A typical example is that of Gerry.

Gerry arrived in my office because he was suffering serious, stress-related, physical problems, including spastic colon, chest pain, vertigo and palpitations. He had all manner of medical tests carried out and was given the all-clear numerous times and yet all these symptoms were making his life a living hell. As we began our work together it was evident that Gerry lived exclusively in the world of the intellect. In our session together I watched him carefully for the subtle and sometimes not so subtle physical clues that some emotional reaction was happening. Every time I saw a physical reaction that gave a clue that there was an emotional reaction such as fear, anger or shame, I questioned him about what he was feeling. Gerry would stop and reflect and would always answer with a thought. He would say something like 'I was thinking about my son's progress in school.' When I pursued it further he would describe something that bothered him about the situation, and eventually after much work he would realise he was angry with his son for his 'laissez-faire' attitude and low grades. For every core emotional state Gerry would have an intellectual analysis that prevented him from experiencing his emotional reactions. The longer we worked together the more he was able to recognise that he was constantly reacting emotionally but could never process or integrate any of these reactions. His early childhood was marked out by emotional sensitivity, a sensitivity that his circumstances at the time had crushed, leaving him almost completely out of touch with his emotional self. As with most men in this condition his body began to react and show the wear and tear of repressed and denied feelings.

A fairly common occurrence for those who work in the fields of therapy and counselling is meeting men who seem to have no feelings. Most end up in therapy consultation rooms in order to try to rescue a marriage that is collapsing or because their children have run amok. Others are suffering the physical manifestations of stress. Most of these are decent, hard-working, honest men who really do not know what people are complaining about. They fit the stereotype of the distant man out of touch with his feelings, who is nowadays often contrasted with the new man, the sensitive, communicative kind that seems made to order for the new millennium. Most of these out-of-touch men are genuine in their attempt to care for the people around them. For many their first adult experience of feelings is grief and fear that they will lose those they value most because they cannot relate at an emotional level.

Frank's story is a good example of the trauma involved in coming to terms with these strange experiences called feelings. After a spell in a treatment centre for addiction to prescription drugs, he gradually began to realise that he had no emotional bonds with anyone. He explained to me that he had what he called chequebook relationships. He married in early adulthood, his wife bore him four children who were now young adults. All through these years he worked hard and tried to solve every problem with money. If there were rows over television programmes, he bought everyone in the house a television; if his wife complained that he was not supportive enough to the family, he hired an extra maid and bought his wife a new car. Because human beings are not designed to live without feelings and because he was completely cut off from his own emotional centre he was able to produce emotional experiences only artificially through drug use. I believe that a crucial element in much of male addictive behaviour is an attempt to replace their damaged emotional functioning with chemically induced emotional states. I will discuss this topic more fully below in the section on sex addiction, here I am drawing attention to the reality that many men go through life cut off from their ability to feel and in so doing create enormous losses for themselves and those they love.

Inappropriate expression of emotions

While a substantial number of men live in unawareness of their emotions a greater number have some connection to their emotional selves intact and can gradually move towards a greater understanding of their importance to a healthy life. These are men who channel their emotional energy into those feelings that men have been traditionally allowed to express — anger, frustration and laughter. It is OK for men to be angry. Their aggressive energy has generally been rewarded. To avoid a fight is, for example, the mark of a coward. To show fear is the mark of a wimp. To curse and swear when something goes wrong is just a man's way to express himself, whereas to cry with a sense of futility is the mark of a 'pussy'. This kind of conditioning leaves many men with a very limited vocabulary when it comes to giving voice to their hearts' concerns. And those close to men sometimes misinterpret the message. So often I see people in my office who describe the reactions of their father or spouse as being that of a bully (and that is exactly how he appears) when on further explorations he is frightened, feels helpless, lost, alone, vulnerable or defeated. Yes, it is understandable that people reject and criticise men who act in an angry and destructive manner. Such rejection, however, often leaves them further defeated and alone.

Most men in these situations have no idea how or why they have come to reflect much that the better part of themselves abhors, and fewer still can track these fault-lines in their character to the way they have been formed from childhood. Robert Bly argues eloquently in *The Sibling Society* that the roots of men's difficulties in emotional expression have a firm hold by the time a boy gets to adolescence.

> As adolescence ends — if there is no effective initiation or mentorship — a sad thing happens. The fire of thinking, the flaring up of creativity, the bonfires of tenderness, all begin to go out. It's as if the Army Corps of Engineers channel wild rivers into concrete banks. This happens to many boys, perhaps most. They become consolidated. They take what is around them, the pulp cutting job, a few local opinions, the drinking culture . . . They feel they have to decide who they are right now. They have no time to feel the trauma; and now that numbing of pain takes over; that numbing often becomes the essence of male life, much more the essence than domination or power over others.

> They adopt their Dad's way of holding it in. They store anger in their bodies, but worse, as John Lee has said over and over, the men do not learn to express anger in a healthy, eloquent or fruitful way. They experience anger but don't know what to do with it. There is a continuum that runs from experiencing anger to expressing it verbally to trying to expel anger from the body through hitting. A man may go as John Lee says from experiencing anger to expelling it in two seconds, skipping over the verbal expression completely and the result for some men will be domestic violence, hitting wives and children.
>
> Most men will not be violent. They will live in this state of expressionless consolidation all their lives, without violence but without spontaneity or creativity either. The numbing of anger and grief will be the primary task of their psyches. The man who remains creative will make art for the rest of his life out of the remnants of infantile and adolescent conflicts. For other men the end of adolescence means a shutting down of expressiveness and a fading of the fires. That is the way it has been for hundreds of years.

Laughter is one form of expression that gives some relief and is readily accessible to men. Sometimes the laughter is a deep belly laugh full of joy and fun; more often, however, laughter is used as a means of disguising other emotions. Listening to the different kinds of male laughter can be an informative experience. So much of their feelings can be reduced and poured through the filter of laughter. Young men mock each other as a means of vying for superiority. This mocking can have deadly impact on some of the recipients. Men laugh at others who are weaker and less competent. Men laugh when they are afraid, men laugh when they are sad. Male laughter like male anger is a kaleidoscope of hidden feelings, easy to misread, and more easily misjudged.

Summary

Many men grow from boyhood to adolescence into manhood with a serious imbalance in their sense of masculinity and their ability to own and express their feelings. This chapter has examined three aspects of distortion. The first is the tough, arrogant and proud, superior and dominant character who sees any form of weakness or vulnerability as a failure of manhood. The second are those that feel defeated in their efforts to be successful enough to believe they are worthwhile men. Some become depressed and dejected, others engage in compensatory activities in order to prove their worth. The third are those that reject their membership of the congregation of men by denying much of their male energy and aspirations, and seek out safety and pleasure as a way of life. Along with these difficulties there is the problem of male emotional impoverishment. None of these forms of being in the world is healthy and each leads to serious difficulties in relationships with other men, with work, with intimacy and with children. The next chapters examine these issues in more detail.

5 Isolation from Other Men

Introduction

One of the most powerful, healing and life-enriching experiences in life is that of close friendship. I well remember as a young boy my mother explaining to me that if I could measure my true friends in life on the fingers of one hand I would be a lucky man. And she was right. As years have gone on the truth of her statement deepens in its impact. To have four or five true friends in a lifetime is a great blessing, and I consider myself privileged in this part of my life. I am particularly fortunate because it is difficult for men in general to cultivate deep friendships. This does not mean that men cannot be loyal, protective, idealistic and a lot else. They can and do develop powerful bonds of commitment and loyalty to one another, they can silently worry about each other's welfare, and go the second, third and fourth miles for each other. They can do all this while missing the actual experience of close friendship. Men can and do die for each other, but most do so without ever having told the other that they love them. The world militates against us knowing how to nourish relationships in general and friendships in particular. This chapter examines some of the difficulties that men encounter in developing friendships that enhance their lives. Three particular barriers to friendship come to mind — the need to compete, the fear of being known, and lack of empathic communication.

The need to compete

Competition often militates against friendship. When we see all our interactions with others as a forum to prove ourselves it is very difficult to relax and get to know someone. When men come together there is an unspoken but very real dynamic in action. The question 'Where do I fit in here?' is constantly at work. The first question most men ask of each other is 'What do you do?' The work identity is then up for evaluation, and the old achievement focus starts to play its part. Men who feel threatened at this stage, those who feel that their work identity is not reflecting enough achievement, begin to explain themselves by saying things like 'It pays the mortgage' or 'It lets me get other things done'. Others who feel more secure in their trade let it lie and still others show off and express pride in their work. Each is, however, doing some kind of evaluation of the other and positions in the pecking order are being established.

Closely related to the nature of the work is the income it provides. Many men evaluate their worth in terms of material success. They identify themselves with the type of car they drive, the clubs they belong to, the leisure activities they engage in. Many men feel intimidated and embarrassed when they find that their masculine marks of achievement and success don't measure up to the others in the group. To outside observers, and especially to many women, this kind of thinking is immature and juvenile, and in many respects it is. One needs to realise, however, that the conditioning that makes men vulnerable to constant vigilance in the presence of other men and sensitive to feeling inadequate is very deep indeed. Thus, in this realm of competition, it is rare to find a professional whose best friend is on welfare, to find the high-ranking civil servant whose close friend is an artist, to find a stressed-out workaholic hanging out with a playful underachiever.

This is not simply a matter of class or taste, it is the outcome of the fact that friendship if anything must be based on respect, and men have been taught that achievement is the forum of respect. Furthermore, achievement in most cases is defined by the values of the wider social context — financial success, prestige, social status, educational achievement, accolade and so on. Men who become redundant or lose their jobs through illness or economic considerations are cut to the core of their identity and often lose not just their sense of dignity but whatever friends they have. Their male friends may find it difficult to associate with those who have become lost and dejected, not simply out of a cruel rejection, but out of a sense of awareness of the other person's difficulty. Without the emotional experience and communication skills necessary to navigate this complex issue some simply withdraw and gradually lose contact.

Men who feel that they have failed to achieve in their working lives find it difficult to be around those who have. And thus the possibilities that exist for some men to develop real friends are limited to those that are their equals in terms of achievement, as defined by society. This is an immediate limitation, not only in terms of the different kind of people one can resource in one's peer group but in terms of the nature of relationships that can evolve. Those who sense that they are disenfranchised and failing can find companionship with others in the same boat, but they are likely to develop friendship based on cynicism. Those of the successful groups develop friendships based on protecting what they have.

Competition puts a barrier between people. Little boys show the competitive spirit from a very young age, the funny yet tragic notions about who can piss higher on the wall or whose penis is bigger are early enactments of who can drive a BMW, take several holidays a year, afford the best colleges for their children. When men compete with each other at this level they have lost the freedom to be themselves and to look at others without judgment, thus failing one of the key elements in friendship, building acceptance.

Fear of vulnerability

Not all men are caught in this competitive web but it is a feature for a great many. A second obstacle to close male friendship is, however, almost universal — namely an inability to share vulnerability. There is an interesting theme that emerges and informs this issue when one examines some of the stories about male friendship. That is the theme of sharing an experience of adversity. Nothing seems to galvanise male friendship and bring it into the realm of true intimacy as much as having shared experience where men have suffered together.

Men who suffer together can build bonds that last a lifetime. Stories of being in warfare are especially common. Much research, for example, shows that those who win the Purple Heart for courage, the Victoria Cross for bravery and all the other types of symbolic prizes for extraordinary feats are not particularly extraordinary men. Nor are they believers in the ideology of whatever war they fight. They are, almost universally, ordinary men catalysed by a devotion and loyalty to the safety of their buddies. When you have vomited in fear in front of your companions, when they see you shit yourself while they wet their pants, there is little left to be said about vulnerability. And most men who read this will know instinctively what it means. Ordinary men do extraordinary things when they find themselves bonded at a soul level to other men. What is rather tragic is that these experiences, those that show the power that inheres in close male bonding, are so rare because they are forced into being rather than chosen. Most men in fact are taught from a very early age not to reveal their tenderness, their hurts, fears and concerns to other men, most are taught not to touch men, to hug them, to tell them that they love them — in fact all the ingredients that are required to nourish friendships are resolutely conditioned out of men from boyhood.

Suffering in the company of other men tears away the façades of overconfidence, competence, independence, strength and all the other hallmarks of machismo, revealing the soft underbelly that lies in the hearts of most men — fears, hurts, tenderness, pity, frailties and weakness. It is only when men are forced to confront vulnerability together, when all they have in the dark night of the soul is the light of each other's compassion, and when the only hope lies in being there for each other, are they able to shrug off the shackles of their learned isolation. And when they do so they can experience profound riches and blessings that can stay with them for a lifetime.

Empathic communication

A third factor that closely relates to the issue of vulnerability is that of empathic communication. Empathy is the ability to understand the feelings of another person. It is not simply an intellectual awareness, but rather a form of emotional identification. Some men reading the passage above will have felt themselves being moved emotionally at the description of male tenderness in the face of adversity. This is a form of empathy.

Men, in general, are not very good at empathy because their conditioning tells them not to waste time trying to understand the nature of another's feelings, but rather to quickly find a way to help him solve his problems. Men can empathise more readily with good feelings than with painful ones. Watching a favourite team playing in championship final is a good example of male empathy. When at the closing minutes that team scores there is an eruption of joy that is shared among the supporters. Men can end up spontaneously hugging each other in this situation, something many would not dream of doing in other, even more appropriate circumstances. Where male empathy is very scarce is when a friend or colleague is troubled. In these circumstances most men are quite inept and often lost. And this is only half the story. Empathy is the internal sense of identification with the other person. Communication is being able to express that experience accurately. And it is here that one can really see some extraordinary levels of well-intentioned but destructive communication. A recent example comes to mind.

Ian is an army officer, and his story is probably the best place to start if one wants to see the failure of both empathy and its communication par excellence. Ian had a nervous breakdown. He was injured in the line of duty although his injury was, like most back injuries, not easily diagnosed and could be mistakenly seen as some form of malingering. He was unable to continue any active work and was consigned to desk duty. He became very depressed as a result, partly because of the consistent pain, partly because he wasn't suited to desk work, and partly because he had lost the respect of his superiors. Soon after these events his wife became tired of his depression and negative frame of mind. She left him and took him to the cleaners financially. A final twist then came when a member of his family got involved in criminal activity and as a result threw a shadow of suspicion on Ian. Within a month his superiors transferred him to a different location where he knew nobody and in doing so announced to him that his career was finished. Ian imploded psychologically. When I met him he had been on suicide watch for a month in a psychiatric hospital, was five stone overweight and could not concentrate to any worthwhile extent because he was on so much medication. To a great extent his life had been destroyed through no fault of his own.

What is particularly relevant to this discussion here is the efforts that his friends made to help Ian during this time. Most of the input involved castigating his wife as a no-good bitch, thus trying to help Ian get over her loss. The other line of approach was to tell him to pull up his socks, get his act together and start going out enjoying himself. With Ian facing profound grief and an almost hopeless set of life circumstances, these approaches to supporting him were worse than useless. And yet they are typical of the responses that men have been taught. Don't look at the feelings, do something, and hope for the best. Most men cannot themselves cope with the feelings of helplessness that emerge when a friend faces such impossible odds. Unfamiliar with the process of giving compassionate support, listening and acknowledging the enormity of the task of surviving this horrible time in his life, his friends end up telling him to do what is impossible. This not only gave no relief, it left him feeling worse and put additional pressure on his friendships.

Empathy is a key element in building an intimate friendship. It is an area where men struggle greatly and have much to learn. It seems appropriate to complete this section with the eloquence of William Doty. He writes:

> To die inwardly for want of a true friend is no less a tragedy today than it has ever been, yet we pay little heed to the cultivation of the friendship arts that may yet save us from a dead end. A truly heroic endeavor might entail not slaughtering dragons so much as taking the first step, and then the second and third steps, toward the friendships that may become for us truly mythical and sustaining.

I believe that empathy is but one of these steps.

Summary

This chapter has briefly examined the ways that men struggle in experiencing true friendship. It advocates the notion that most men have within them both the desire and the potential to build bonds of love and loyalty that are of extraordinary value. Many can only access these experiences when forced, through mutual experiences of suffering, to let down the barriers that keep men isolated from each other. These barriers are constructed in boys as part of their formation and include unnecessary competition, fear of vulnerability and difficulties with empathy.

6 Dysfunctional Relationship to Work

Introduction

Another area that causes men to suffer as a result of their formation is the way they relate to work. Achievement is a defining element of male self-image and self-worth. Work is the modern-day forum for this aspect of male identity. Formerly, in the warrior time, physical prowess was a key element. The growth of technology, built on top of the industrial machine, has now made warriors obsolete. In any modern-day warfare, a platoon of fit and ardent warriors can be taken out by a computer nerd 500 miles away at the push of a button. Today's warriors are in the world of business. And some could argue that today's world is business. It is almost twenty-five years since the film *Network* brilliantly portrayed the role of big business in the structure of our world. The hero, Howard Beale, is savaged by his boss thus:

> You get up on your little twenty-one-inch screen and howl about democracy and America. There is no America. There is no democracy. There is only IBM, ITT and AT&T and Du Pont, Dow and Union Carbide, Exxon. Those are the nations of the world today . . . We no longer live in a world of nations and ideologies, Mr Beale. The world is a college of corporations, inexorably determined by the immutable by-laws of business. The world is a business, Mr Beale. It has been since man crawled out of the slime.

If the world is a business, it is men who are the main sustainers through their overidentification with their work. When we examine the way that men relate to work we discover that many suffer greatly in terms of their emotional health by virtue of the form that the relationship takes. Two common ailments are direct outcomes from male identification with work as the basis for self-worth. These could be termed the erosion of the self, and the corporate cult.

The erosion of the self

If work is the forum for male self-expression it disenfranchises most who enter the fray. The marginal few that can see real achievement in their work are far outnumbered by those for whom work is a daily trial of endurance. In general, we see the emotional bond between men and work as a formula for serious levels of ill health. If men are valued in terms of their achievement they can find themselves in one of two predicaments. First, and more commonly, they are trapped in a job that uses up most of their energy and offers little by way of dignity, creativity or meaning. For these men the options are limited to seeing their daily toil as a necessary sacrifice in order to fulfil their mandate as men and provide for their families. Bruce Springsteen can be seen as the poet of the disenfranchised men of working-class America, his lyrics are haunting in their resonance and express far better than I can the depth of despair that can inhere in men's loss of dignity and meaning in work.

> You're born into this life paying
> for the sins of somebody else's past,
> Daddy worked his whole life for nothing
> but the pain
> Now he walks these empty rooms,
> looking for something to blame,
> You inherit the sins, you inherit the flames
> Adam raised a Cain

Such lyrics carry deep meaning for those who have been touched by the ennui and alienation that many men suffer. For a lot of such men their emotional needs are met through some kind of fellowship with workmates who are in the same struggle. Given men's difficulty in revealing their vulnerabilities and struggles the limit of the nourishment they get from other men is to laugh together at those in authority, play games in the pub, give out about their spouses and enjoy each other's competitiveness around sport.

The enormous interest in club sports such as football leagues is a testament to the need men have to find some source of attachment of meaning because of the emptiness they experience in their own working lives. A love of sport is not in itself symptomatic of unhappiness. What is more interesting is the bond that is built between men and particular teams, a passion that often surpasses their love for the game itself. Millions come together in small groups at weekends to sit and watch the symbolic battles being fought between their tribe and the enemy. The grace and athleticism, the style, passion and beauty involved in the energy of these young players stir primal forces in many men. They shout, cheer and even cry at times at the glory of winning and the despair of defeat. Given that there is such a drought in men's opportunity to bond with each other there is much value in such communion. As one great soccer manager is often quoted as saying, 'Some people think football is a matter of life and death . . . it is much more serious than that.'

It is difficult for men whose productive energies are being used up by the industrial machine or the administrative infrastructure to find the energy to develop alternative activities that could help them express their creativity. To do so requires money, opportunities and energy, but perhaps more importantly it requires awareness. For many these are luxuries. They can, however, find an outlet by emotionally engaging with their favourite team and enjoying the emotional connection through the competition with other men. The joy and excitement that is felt as a result of this communion with other men is never directly talked about, for to talk of such things is for most men taboo, but it works and is a salve and a comfort to a great many who otherwise are locked emotionally into a place of isolation and aloneness.

The corporate cult

A second predicament is found among those whose work allows a large measure of visible success, financial reward and the expression of power. These men are the leaders in the world of work. They may find themselves in managerial positions in industry or in a decision making capacity in the white-collar service industries. Many are enthusiastic and most are blinkered in their commitment and zeal regarding their work. There is profound danger to many men lurking at the centre of much of the corporate machine. As we have seen above men are conditioned to experience their self-worth and dignity by what they produce and achieve. This is a very serious weakness in the psychological structure of men and leads many into an emotional and, in some instances, an actual early grave.

Once a person has attached their self-esteem to a particular activity or relationship they can easily become a hostage to that activity or that relationship. The corporate machine has a built-in awareness of this vulnerability in men and has mechanisms in place by which to exploit this to the full. Some of these are based on decades of research by psychologists into the nature of motivation. Men, for the most part, become involved in the corporate machine when they first begin work. Most end up in the predicament described above, but a few are chosen because they have extraordinary potential, talent, skill, education or personality. These are the elite that become identified with the organisation rather than simply working for it. They have made a subtle but important psychological shift. They have become believers in the organisation. Their identity has become connected to the organisation. And this is, in fact, recognised by organisations to be an essential requirement of the employee who becomes part of the bigger picture, it is called loyalty, commitment, becoming a company man.

In return for this soul commitment the man is offered financial reward but, far more importantly for men, a sense of having succeeded, of beating the competition, of having pride. This latter driving force is very effective for men and is in its essence dysfunctional. It is in C.S. Lewis's words — the magician's bargain — 'Give up our soul, get power in return. But once our souls, that is our selves, have been given up, the power thus conferred will not belong to us. We shall in fact be the slaves and puppets of that to which we have given our souls.' If codependency (a form of addictive dysfunctional relationship) is the great psychological disorder suffered by many women, becoming a member of the corporate cult is its parallel in the lives of men.

I use the term corporate cult because there are certain features of this disorder that resemble what is known of the profoundly damaging and intractable nature of how religious cult members are affected. At base there is an ideology. Religious cults have a vast array of them, from being saved by aliens to being raptured into heaven during the second coming of Christ. Corporate ideology is pretty similar from one organisation to another. It's about profit, and winning. One is intrinsically linked to the other.

There is an out-group, all religious cults can easily identify them, namely those who do not believe in the ideology. In the corporate cult the out-group are the competitor, those that have failed, the wimps, the do-gooders, or simply the ones on lower rungs of the ladder who have no power.

There is an elite. Religious cults have a certain member who is the guru, other members may be seen as the elders, or closer to the guru or enlightenment or whatever. In the corporate cult there are the movers and shakers. These are endowed by those who look up to them with qualities they may not in reality possess.

There are rituals. In religious cults these are understood and accepted and their function is to reinforce the structure of the cult and to keep the members tightly bound to the ideology and to each other. In the corporate cult these rituals are less apparent — company barbecues, who gets to sit nearest the top table at company outings, training days designed to enhance the *esprit de corps* and so on.

And perhaps most importantly because it is the central element in keeping the system working, there is an emotional bond that involves surrender of critical faculties. In old-fashioned terms this is called brainwashing. Religious cult members rationalise inconsistencies and deny losses and problems that are directly related to being members of the cult. These can include the loss of a balanced life, of family relationships, of health and happiness. In the corporate cult the members deny the reality that they are being used, that they have not found a new family, that they will get tired and old, and new, more aggressive young ones will take their place. They are disposable, they will eventually become redundant and ultimately the corporation does not care about them.

It is important here to clarify that not all people who work in management level or positions of power are cult members. Some realise that their work is a job that may or may not contain high levels of satisfaction and creativity. Financial rewards and other compensations are exchanged for one's talents, energy and ideas. This exchange is the basis for a healthy relationship to one's work and some manage to attain this balance. In many instances where a person realises this he must pretend to be more emotionally bonded to the corporation than he is in reality. When it is noted that he is not a 'company man' he may find himself being left behind in the promotion race, and overtaken by those who are prepared to make a higher level of commitment. Men are cultivated and trained to look around the world to find something that tells them that they are a success. Most do not look to relationships for this affirmation and are thus very vulnerable to the corporate cult.

Terry is a victim of the corporate cult. He sits in front of me with his face in his hands. Already his body language communicates the shame he feels at the deepest part of himself. He is in his mid-forties, the time of real testing for a career in terms of whether or not one has reached the end of the line in an organisation. Terry's life is devastated. As a young man in his early twenties he was wide-eyed, idealistic and impressionable. He rose quickly in the ranks of a large financial service organisation. He opened his home to the young recruits coming up behind him, talked to them about their fears and feelings of inadequacy, and taught them all he knew. He awoke in the morning proud to be himself, togged out in the requisite suit and tie, drove his nice car from his upper-middle-class house into work. He lived for his work and gained a great deal of self-esteem through it.

Then one day he was called into the head office and told that as a result of restructuring his job was being discarded. He could take a settlement or retrain into work three steps down the ladder while remaining at the same pay level subject to target achievement. His early shock at the news was replaced by efforts to carve out a better deal that would allow him to maintain some of the nature of the work he was already doing and some of the title and prestige attached. For several months Terry believed that the organisation did not really understand what was happening to him. When it finally dawned on him that it did not really care and that he was dispensable, Terry had a nervous breakdown. Terry was the kind of man that would never darken the door of a therapist's office. He was a man of fairly simple outlook. From humble origins and a hard-working traditional family, he had put himself on the map, had the respect of his family and a clear picture as to how his life would work out. Little did he know that the structure of his personality carried within it a serious fault-line that caused him to implode psychologically when the basis of his security was taken away.

It is a general principle of psychological health that the greater the dependence for our well-being that we place on circumstances outside our control, the greater our vulnerability when they go awry. In the first session with Terry I said something that he continued to rely on throughout the year of therapy that ensued. I said in summarising the root of his distress, 'Terry, they gave you a job, you gave them a core part of your life, when they took the job away they took part of you with it.' Our work together then focused on how and why this man gave so much of himself to an organisation that, truth be told, didn't ask for it. Terry's recovery was painful but, in hindsight, he believes that it was worth it. He had no idea that his life was built on sand, that he had completely constricted himself, given up on many aspects of himself, had an arid relationship with his spouse, a shallow relationship with his children. All of this was exposed through the trauma, and in his case would never have seen the light of day otherwise. His breakdown was, in essence, a breakthrough.

Terry's story has a happy ending. Most of these situations don't. Many men do not have the traumatic amputation that Terry suffered; rather, there is a growing realisation that they are being selected out in the Darwinistic process of survival of the fittest. Some recent films portray the poignancy of this awful dawning, one of the best being *Glengarry Glen Ross*. Aside from containing passages of extraordinary acting by Jack Lemmon and Al Pacino, it is searing in its examination of the desperation that surfaces in many men when they face into the decline of their achievement and pride based on a dysfunctional relationship with work. The film should be required watching for all the young men who enter management or target-based professions. They can get a glimpse of what is going to happen to them if they tie themselves emotionally to any prestige or esteem granted by an organisation.

Another aspect of this process is the cult of youthism in the work environment, nicely reflected by comparing an older film,

Kramer vs. Kramer, with the recent *Jerry Maguire*. In the former, released in 1979, the main character played by Dustin Hoffman is recently divorced and is caring full-time for his young son. This new level of responsibility has a serious impact on his ability to continue with his high level of commitment to his work. As a result his boss takes him to lunch, tells him that he is to lose his job and offers him a large severance pay package. In this scene there is some sense of dignity in the attempts made to break the news gently and there is a sense of compassion on the part of the boss, an older man. In *Jerry Maguire* we see the character played by Tom Cruise, an arrogant confident player in the company, take a traumatic fall from grace. He has not reached his targets and is fired swiftly and ruthlessly by an underling, a guy whom he despises and who appeared to be lower in the pecking order.

The difference in these films shows the progression of ruthlessness that is at the heart of corporate business. I myself am not so concerned about this as a matter of commercial reality. Any society that has as its central economic activity a reliance on profit-oriented capitalism must pay a certain price. Thus far there seem to be few alternatives that can succeed as a way for human beings to live and work together, and I believe that there are enormous successes and advantages to this as an economic system. I am more concerned that most men do not realise the aggression and cruelty that is implicit in this system. They are taken in by their own competitive pride, and blinded by the illusions created by human resources ideology. Those who get close to the heart of corporate capitalism know that 'business is war'. To the winner go the spoils and the losers just disappear.

In this context men can be very cruel to each other. The moment weakness is spotted it is removed. Men who are not making the grade suddenly find that they are not invited to social outings, those facing the drop are neglected or looked upon with some version of pity that is as undignified as it is insincere. The men around these lost ones become afraid for themselves.

Beneath the surface they worry that if this can happen to someone they know then it can happen to them. The film *Wall Street* captures the cruelty that emerges in these situations. A subtheme portrays the attitude of the young and eager fighters towards an older employee who no longer has the strength or belief to stay fighting. He is eventually 'put out to grass' and the film's central character comments to his colleague that he'd better get on with it or he will end up like this unfortunate man.

In military conflict soldiers have their limbs shot off, some are crippled for life, others lose their lives and still others live in trauma for the rest of their days. Most know that this is the reality of war, even if they do not truly appreciate its meaning. It is not very different in corporate capitalism. The scars and wounds are to the ego, to financial security, to family life, to emotional health. Most men become victims of this system without any insight into what has happened to them. While most of those who become aware that they are being damaged can do little about it, they at least have the option to minimise that damage and compensate in some ways for what they are losing.

Summary

This chapter has examined the way that formative influences in cultivating young boys encourage them to identify too closely with work as the basis for self-esteem. As a result there is a deep sense of inadequacy and defeat among many men when they spend their productive energies in work that has few rewards and little meaning. A second difficulty is found among those men who are very successful and who also identify their value with this success. In doing so they lose perspective and either burn out or lose themselves in the process. Work is important and valuable, being productive and creative, taking responsibility to earn and provide for one's dependants are virtues worthy of pursuit, but the value of one's self can never be tied to these without serious consequences for one's health and happiness.

7 Impoverished Relationships with Women

Introduction

Most men want to experience love, tenderness and companionship in an intimate relationship with a woman. I have used the term impoverished here to explain that, in spite of their heartfelt wishes, a great many men relate to women in such a way that they and their partners become impoverished rather than enriched through the experience. In this chapter I will examine some of the key reasons why so many men seem unable to reach the goal of intimate relationships in their lives.

The history of human relationships suggests that men have always experienced some confusion and difficulty in building healthy relationships with women. The capacity to enjoy the friendship of women, to avoid unnecessary pain from them, to be aware that some women are dangerous while others are life-enriching, to cultivate those friendships that can enhance one's own life, to respect and receive respect in equal measure are areas that seem central to healthy relationships. These are the kinds of evaluations most men make when interacting with each other. When it comes to relating to women there appears to be some unconscious switch that changes the rules. This is not simply in relation to sexual attraction, which even further confuses the issue. Inside every man there seems to be a code that tells him that women are to be treated in a particular way and this code seems heavily influenced by cultural taboos and mores as well as by early formative childhood experiences.

We have seen above that one of the most influential factors in men's attitudes and behaviour to women is the vestiges that remain from when women were seen as property, as weaker vessels to be protected. This creates an immediate sense of inequality when boys grow up into young men who wish to relate to women. A second and to my mind even more profoundly influential force is the tearing of boys away from the world of the feminine at a young age. I discussed this earlier as a process that is undertaken in order to make tougher characters. Here I wish to examine its impact on men as they begin to relate to women.

Damaging a boy's sensitivity and feelings so as to repress or curtail what can be termed his feminine self creates a deep loss within him psychologically. For evermore he is incomplete. It seems a logical step to then conclude that this young man begins to see in the feminine a lost part of himself. The vast majority of men have no conscious awareness that this is what is happening to them when they seek to have their needs met through a relationship with a woman. In so far as men seek to complete their own damaged identities through relating to women they burden relationships with an inappropriate task from the very beginning. Additionally, the emotions that are aroused in this encounter are of primal intensity, because they belong to the instinctual early childhood part of the psyche. As a consequence they become dangerous when acted out by adults, and this may go some way to explain the levels of violence and abuse that are seen between men and women who supposedly love each other. Furthermore, and despite popular opinion, men take longer to de-love women when relationships come to an end. This may be because the loss of the relationship may be a re-injury to the earlier wound where the man lost part of himself. Men's heartbreak seems to run as deep and in many cases to run deeper when love is lost, although it may be better hidden or transferred into some dysfunctional acting out behaviour. This covert and disguised form of dealing with the pain of loss is a direct result of treating boys in ways that cauterise them emotionally so that they do not, in general, know how to grieve in a healthy and healing way when they become adults.

These two formidable forces, an imbalance in the equality of relationship, and profound need to reconnect with the feminine, lie deep in the psyche of most men and emerge and reactivate when they begin to pursue intimate relationships with women. These forces create problems and many such relationships are, therefore, in difficulty from the beginning. In general, several types of dysfunction can occur as a result of these forces. I have summarised these under four headings: (i) idealisation, (ii) oppression, (iii) objectification and (iv) submission.

(i) Idealisation

Idealisation in the context of male-female relationship refers to the psychological process whereby a man creates a frame for his attitudes to and feelings for women that is unrealistic and inaccurate. Women are seen as having certain features that make them almost untouchable. In general, they are seen as kind, mysterious, asexual and aloof. The man has denied the possibility of a dark side in the feminine.

History tells us that women are not morally superior to men, that they are capable of cruelty as well as love, of jealous vindictiveness as well as kind-hearted care, of competitive rivalry as well as gracious humility. Idealisation is the failure to either see or accept this reality. The best example of this as a widespread cultural phenomenon is the worship of the Madonna. From the twelfth century onwards as the development of the church put an end to the Dark Ages and provided what can be considered the foundation for Western civilisation, the figure of the Madonna became established as an important icon of worship. Despite the fact that the church was almost wholly run by men, there was an obvious need within the human family to elevate a woman into some idealistic state.

I like Kenneth Clark's commentary on this cultural conditioning. In *Civilisation* he writes:

> Of the two or three faculties that have been added to the European mind since the civilisation of Greece and Rome, none seems to me stranger and more inexplicable than the sentiment of ideal or courtly love. It was entirely unknown to antiquity. Passion, yes; desire, yes of course; steady affection; yes. But this state of utter subjection to the will of an almost unapproachable woman; this belief that no sacrifice was too great, that a whole lifetime might properly be spent in paying court to some exacting lady or suffering on her behalf — this would have seemed to the Romans or to the Vikings not only absurd but unbelievable; and yet for hundreds of years it passed unquestioned. It inspired a vast literature . . . and even up to 1945 we still retained a number of chivalrous gestures; we raised our hats to ladies, and let them pass first through doors, and, in America, pushed in their seats at table. And we still subscribed to the fantasy that they were chaste and pure beings, in whose presence we couldn't tell certain stories or pronounce certain words. Well that's all over now, but it had a long run, and there was something to be said for it.

I'm not sure that it is all over now. I believe that many men have deep in their interior a tendency to idealise women. In this culture this has been reinforced significantly by the worship of the Madonna. In the nature of honouring the idealised female figure certain themes emerge. She is sexless. In the midst of one's prayers to the Virgin, it is difficult to imagine the likely scene of Mary the mother of Jesus having a complete human relationship with Joseph. Imagine her waiting for Joseph to get back from some carpentry job, fixing a cartwheel, making a door or whatever. He arrives back and finds Mary tending some vegetables in their little plot. She looks great, he follows her out to the garden and gives her a drink of spring water. They look at each other with that look and retire up to the loft for a sensual, erotic and pleasurable romp. It can play havoc with one's religious practice to imagine that scene while praying to the Madonna for a miraculous intervention.

Sexual shame and idealisation

Idealisation is most clearly seen in the realm of sexual desire. For some men idealising women means seeing them as not wanting or needing a sexual relationship. Built into such idealisation is usually some shame around one's own masculine sexuality. Andrew Stanway in *The Complete Book of Love and Sex* makes the interesting argument that some boys cope with their sexual attraction to their mothers by projecting onto them a sexless nature. Later in life these boys become men who see themselves as lustful and selfish because of the stridency of their sexual urges, whereas women retain the sexlessness of mother. This form of dysfunctional relationship leads to deep unhappiness and shame. These men are more likely to choose women who have sexual problems, particularly of a developmental nature. Some women under the cultural conditioning of the idealised female grow to repress and deny their own sexuality. They become prudish and uncomfortable with the physicality of sex, preferring to keep some romanticised notion of spiritualised sex rather than the very raw reality of bodily encounter as an expression of intimate love and giving and receiving pleasure.

I was recently confronted on this issue. After a seminar on relationships one of the women in the group asked the simple question, 'Michael, in regard to men's interest in women, does it always start with lust?' This lady's body language, voice tone, facial expressions and eye contact all communicated to me that she had had some serious trouble with men, and certainly didn't like what she saw as their predatory sexual nature. I thought for a moment and said that in most cases where men are sexually interested in women it starts with desire. Men who idealise women believe that this desire is not reciprocated, and tend to choose dysfunctional female partners as a result. And thus the cycle continues.

This problem is quite common, even in an age of such sexual liberation. I have had therapeutic conversations with a significant number of men over the years who wish that they could rid themselves of their sexual drive. Some cause themselves enormous distress by visiting prostitutes. They feel that in some weird way they are protecting their innocent wives from their crude sexual desires by dissipating themselves elsewhere. Then they are left with the torment and guilt and further reinforce their sense of sexual shame. The fact that most are normal healthy men in their sexuality is of cold comfort to them, so deeply ingrained is their belief that to express their sexual needs in a relationship is to somehow defile a beauty or innocence in the women they love.

Others cope by sublimating their sexual desires into physical activity, or into intense religious practice. I have long held the view that some of the more excessive practices of inflicting pain on oneself for the sake of becoming more spiritually pure were and are a form of sexual sublimation. It is perhaps no coincidence that the Middle Ages witnessed both the high point of Madonna worship and the widespread practice of a variety of different forms of self-flagellation.

When men idealise women they give great weight and value to the characteristics that women develop as part of their formative experiences as females. Women, for example, are in general more emotionally expressive and more articulate and pay attention to details that men often miss. They are not as overtly aggressive or apparently competitive. These characteristics are often mistaken as having greater virtue than the qualities that men possess, such as single-mindedness or silent appraisal. The differences between men and women are in fact a matter of style and are morally neutral.

Female cruelty and idealisation

When women act in an evil way they do it differently to men. If a woman wants somebody hurt then she is more likely to strike at the heart emotionally through some verbal assault. Inflicting emotional pain is morally as reprehensible as other forms of destructive behaviour. If a woman wishes to see someone physically hurt she is more likely to get a man to do the deed for her. Most contract killers are men, a substantial number of their customers are women. If, for example, a woman is greatly angry with a spouse for the break-up of a relationship, she can find a myriad of ways to be supported in her desire for vengeance, usually by trying to break him financially. In the film *The First Wives Club* we hear the punchline, 'Don't get mad, get everything.' In many instances women can use the legal profession far more effectively in damaging a wayward spouse. Those sympathetic male judges who also idealise women often play the role of surrogate husbands.

History tells us that female cruelty is just as damaging as that of males. From Queen Hatshepsut to Cleopatra, the mythical queen Meadbh of Connacht to Granuaille, from Mary Queen of Scots to Elizabeth the Great, from Indira Gandhi to Imelda Marcos, women in power have misused it just as destructively as men when it suited their ends. When I hear arguments that favour women as more peaceable creatures I think of the hundreds of young Argentinian sailors doomed to a watery grave while their ship the *Belgrano* sped as fast as possible away from the exclusion zone around the Falkland Islands, all on the political whim of Margaret Thatcher. The bitter pill of female cruelty may look and taste different but it is just as lethal.

Idealising women involves seeing them as sophisticated and morally superior. Men who do so are at risk of being used and abused by women who, in certain instances, can see the man's blind spot and use it to their ends. I have had many conversations with women who exclaim wonderment at some men that they admire who marry most difficult and often emotionally destructive women. These astute female observers sometimes ask, 'How is it that the real bitches always get the good men?' Thinking about this issue one can see that in these situations it is almost always a failure on the part of the man to understand that women can act with great self-centredness and dress up their use of a man under the guise of love.

The opposite process, men damaging women, is also very prevalent and has been addressed in numerous books. This occurs when women enter very destructive relationships with problematic, immature and sometimes dangerous men. There is, however, one major difference in this situation. In most cases the woman knows that the man is damaged, she rationalises the relationship by focusing on the quality of her love, and hopes that with enough of it he will change. When a good man finds himself in a relationship with a dangerous woman the focus is not on the quality of his love, rather it is on denying the reality of the nature of his partner. Idealisation is but one form of dysfunctional relationship with women, oppression is another.

(ii) Oppression

Once we engage in the important topic of men oppressing women we enter a minefield. There is so much anger and intensely held opinion on the matter that the topic has the potential to be explosive. The reader will recall my rather sobering experience in discussing the rite of marriage and the ritual of the father of the bride 'giving away' his daughter. The intensity of reaction to this one small event in the whole structure of male-female relationships is indicative of the strength of the views held about such matters. That conversation and much experience since then has informed me of the risks inherent in any man discussing the nature of oppression between men and women. And yet if men are to understand anything of our own issues around how we relate to women then we must reach some informed understanding of why some men oppress women. I will leave it to a female author to undertake an analysis about the ways that women damage men.

Additionally, we must set some limits on this discussion because there is enough breadth and complexity here to require the remainder of the book. We could examine this area under a variety of lenses: the lens of politically motivated oppression, the lens of economic oppression, the lens of sociological movements and cultural trends, and so on. In the present context I wish to explore the reasons that some men oppress women as a direct result of their conditioning and training within their families, reinforced by society. Before doing so I would like to present some brief comment on the general picture of the oppression of women throughout the ages.

Historical precedent for oppression

As a starting point I would like to cite a historian referred to by Susan Bordo in an article entitled 'Feminism, postmodernism, and gender skepticism'. She writes, 'In 1987, I heard a feminist historian claim that there were absolutely no common areas of experience between the wife of a plantation owner in the pre-civil war South and the female slaves her husband owned.' Gender, she argued, is so thoroughly fragmented by race, class, historical particularity and individual difference as to be useless as an analytical category. The 'bonds of womanhood', she insisted, 'are a feminist fantasy born out of the ethnocentricity of white middle-class academics'. While this is strong language and does not reflect Bordo's own viewpoint, it seems to me to carry much weight when it comes to understanding the issue of oppression in a historical context.

Historical accounts from the earliest days show one thing clearly: in the human family those in power use those they can overpower for their own ends. Altruism and compassion are noticed when they feature because they are not the general characteristics of the way that people relate to each other. Furthermore, in nearly all cases the rules of 'civilised' conduct are confined to a variety of elitist minorities that change over time. We have also seen that slavery is a characteristic of human history well into this century, if we include the enslavement of the Jews under Hitler as well as the less well-documented slavery of the Gulags in Russia. Owning people, abusing them, treating them according to a different set of rules is a feature of human history and importantly the elite who carried out this oppression in all cases were made up of both sexes. The women who were married to the plantation owners may not have engaged in sex in the barn to the same extent as their husbands (not necessarily out of modesty or virtue but for fear of bearing a mixed-blood child) but their use of slaves as field hands, nursemaids and domestics is clearly a part of the oppression of women and men by the white female elite of that time.

The German women who adhered to the theory of Aryan superiority and bore beautiful blond blue-eyed Germans with the specific goal of continuing the expansion and furthering the aims of the Third Reich are no less culpable of oppression than the civil servants who wrote the train timetables for the transport of Jews to the death camps. I think it is time to begin to see oppression as a feature of human history born out of ignorance, desperation, economic competition and so on. Sam Keen is eloquent and effective in presenting this viewpoint. He says in reference to the notion that the history of humanity is a history of the oppression of women:

> This type of demonic history renders men responsible for all the ills of society, and women innocent. If there is warfare it is because men are naturally hostile and warlike, not because when tribes and peoples come into conflict it is the males who have been historically conditioned, trained and expected to fulfil the role of warrior. If there is environmental pollution it is not because it is the inevitable result of the urban-technological-industrial lifestyle that modern people have chosen, but because of patriarchal technology . . . And if there is injustice in society it is not

> because some men and some women are insensitive to the sufferings of others but because white male oppressors dominate all women and people of colour . . . The notion that women are a class or a repressed minority like migrant workers, blacks, Indians in America or Jews in Germany, trivialises the pain involved in class structure and the systematic abuse suffered by ethnic minorities. The injustices that go with class and race are too severe to be confused with the gender problem. All upper classes are composed of equal numbers of men and women. The fruits of exploitation are enjoyed equally by men, women and children of the upper classes as the outrages of exploitation are borne equally by men, women and children of the lower classes. Both classes and ethnic minorities suffer real oppression . . . It is an insult to the oppressed of the world to have rich and powerful women included within the congregation of the downtrodden merely because they are female.

So, where does that leave us in relation to men oppressing women? We can no longer rely on some historical precedent to make sense of this. Let us consider what it means for a man to oppress a woman.

De-selfing women through oppression

A dysfunctional relationship that involves such oppression can be usefully described as having as its objective the de-selfing of the woman. The relationship dynamic includes behaviours and communication that gradually undermine the woman, erode her self-confidence, prevent her from knowing and actualising her creative and productive energies. In general, it also has an economic aspect that impoverishes her, leaving her more vulnerable to the continuing destruction of her identity. Why would a man want to do this to a woman? Radical feminists argue that it is what most men want. I disagree. I believe that most men want a relationship that assures them that they are loved and respected, in which their sexual needs will be met and they will enjoy the companionship of their partner. Relatively few actually achieve this and some end up causing great harm to the woman that they choose.

Some men are downright evil and destructive, as are some women, and will therefore hurt everybody they can, including women. This situation is not under discussion here as the roots of such generalised hatred and violence are too broad to be encompassed. Rather our focus is on those men who reserve oppressive treatment for adult women, and who otherwise are decent and kind to others and to their children. Men who oppress women in this way are often unconscious of the forces that drive them to negate and erode their partners. In my experience of working with men who have resolutely demolished the identity and self-esteem of their women over decades, there are several features, the first being fear. Men who hurt women in this way are almost always afraid of the power that is incubating in the feminine. The woman in the situation is representative of the feminine energy and the male is primordially afraid of this power. He defuses the power by destroying the carrier. This is, of course, no excuse for destructive behaviour, but without understanding it we are left with clichés and meaningless generalisations that are essentially simply name-calling — 'male chauvinist pigs', 'all men are bastards' and so on.

Why are some men afraid of the power of the feminine? One possible answer for men is that the earliest and most fundamental experience in life is helplessness in the hands of a woman. The right to life or death lay in the hands of his mother. Later in childhood the rights to love and affection, nourishment, self-worth and self-esteem all began in that primal relationship. In some situations the mother has been cruel, unkind, punitive or neglectful and has thus created a dependency in the young boy by virtue of not adequately meeting his developmental needs.

Such inadequate or deficient mothering is not, however, always to blame in men mistreating women in adult life. For some the very nature of the effect of a woman's love can cause a deep fear reaction. As a man matures out of the boyhood and adolescent years, his desire for connection, his powerful sexual drive and in most instances his damaged emotions seek consolation and healing in the arms of a woman. That kind of vulnerability is too much for some men. And because they despise their own vulnerability (and have learned to do so throughout boyhood) they lash out at anyone who brings it to the fore. The woman's capacity to locate a man's vulnerability makes her very dangerous to those who cannot cope with its exposure. Some men then resort to hurting their loved one to keep her at bay. This is but one strand, further enhanced in its capacity to wound by the second underlying emotion, anger.

Oppression and male anger

Some men are angry with the feminine. We have seen earlier that there is an implicit unfairness in the treatment of boys and girls in their formative years. This affects both differently and both have scars that linger in later life. In men, anger is an emotion that is allowed and often encouraged in some form of competitive activity during the formative years. Many men are angry as a result of the failures and difficulties that are encountered in their attempts to become an acceptable person, or more accurately an acceptable man. They cannot express the upset, grief and fear that are at most times associated with these personal difficulties. But they can get angry. It is in the nature of anger to become displaced onto people who hold least threat. Displacement is a defence mechanism that is commonly used by people dealing with their anger. One of the best-known descriptions is that of a man who is in trouble at work, comes home and takes it out on his wife, she in turn gets cross with her child who in turn goes out and kicks the cat. If we add together these two parts — anger being one of the few emotions men can identify and express, and the strategy of displacement — we can see that for some men there is a habitual tendency to vent their anger onto their partner.

In many instances where men are displacing their anger they do not realise that this is what is happening. Once again the difficulty in understanding their own emotional make-up, which is a direct result of their formative training, becomes an obstacle to developing a healthy relationship. A man may see that his partner's forgetfulness about a telephone message is actually the cause of the anger when it isn't. His growing resentment may be stewing beneath the surface just waiting for some excuse to allow it to explode. Some of this resentment may be an accumulation of the frustration and sense of failure that characterise many men's relationship to work as discussed above. When the man's anger erupts in an inappropriate context neither partner realises the nature of these conflicts and sometimes the woman believes that his anger is actually related to whatever flaw in her he has targeted. She believes that he is annoyed with her, thus cultivating a negative self-concept, namely that there is nothing she can do right. The constant attrition that characterises some relationships eventually can destroy the woman's self-image, leaving her broken and humiliated.

Oppression and male fear

A third strand that seems to be a feature of relationships whereby men oppress women relates to that well-known but little-understood organ, the male ego. We have seen earlier that men are cultivated and conditioned to believe that their worth is based on their sense of success and achievement. For some men this is particularly intense when it comes to proving one's abilities in the eyes of a woman.

In my discussions with women about this issue, I have heard of an especially effective ploy to engage a man's interest that specifically targets this need. I have heard it called the 'awe treatment'. The rules are simple — if you want a man to like you or pursue you then give him the awe treatment: when he is talking look interested, when he jokes laugh a little longer than is necessary, look somewhat impressed and tell him he is very interesting. Most men I talk to tell me that this really works. It is clear therefore that many women understand the desire most men feel to be a success in their eyes. For men it is often an unconscious drive, ingrained since those wonderful smiles of mother when he made her proud. Basing some of her self-worth on his success and achievement, she plants the seed of his need to be worthy of a woman's respect. This dynamic can of course be a really positive part of a healthy relationship. There is, however, a downside. It sets up a situation where to fail in the eyes of a woman is a deeply felt wound. This means that some men are unable to cope if they feel a failure in the eyes of a woman, and more especially a woman that they love. These men become competitive with women. They cannot bear that a woman could be better at something than they are. When a man such as this gets into a relationship with a woman, an unspoken part of the script is that she not better him in any way. In its most intense form the man who operates from this place is the typical male chauvinist pig. He will spurn her and ridicule her at every turn rather than admit that he feels he is not good enough for her. Anne Dickson is particularly insightful into this aspect when she writes in *The Mirror Within*:

> A man is vulnerable to a deep fear linked to the constant push to be master of himself, his body, other people, the world. The fact that mastery is impossible ultimately simply increases the fear of exposure. This is compounded further, in many men, by a deep mistrust of women, so the fear remains locked away and emerges only as aggression.

It is very painful to watch men who have lived out their relationships in this manner come to terms with the damage they have done. Certain men can engage their spouse in some form of healing and in most cases the woman is shocked to learn that beneath all the ridicule and bravado he is intimidated by her. It is rare that the relationship survives long enough for healing to begin.

When we put these three strands together, fear of being overpowered and of one's vulnerability being accessed, with anger from other situations being displaced onto the easiest available target, alongside repressed feelings of inferiority or intimidation, we have a powerfully destructive cocktail that leads to deep and chronic erosion of a woman's self-esteem at the hands of such men.

(iii) Objectification

Objectification means treating a person as an object, using a person for one's own ends with no regard for the value or wishes of the person. When we take this broader view we realise that men and women have been objectified for centuries. Industrial psychology went to great lengths to explain to the industrial machine that human beings cannot simply be treated as a pair of hands, eyes or legs (ironically, these studies were often used to increase motivation to get those legs and hands working faster). Most of the early factory complexes simply used the physical strength of people with no regard for their health, safety or quality of life, and most of these were men. The military complex is perhaps the clearest example of objectification. Its whole *raison d'être* is to use young men's bodies and minds as expendable commodities. A viewing of the recent film *Saving Private Ryan* is a powerful and graphic reminder of the objectification of young men. And the reality is that in this case, the invasion of Normandy was a necessary step in protecting the Western world from the great evil threatening it at that time.

Prostitution

Perhaps the most well-documented and clearly stated example of objectification is that of prostitution. Much has been written on this topic from the viewpoint of feminist ideology, some of the most reactionary and frightening work by the radical feminist Andrea Dworkin. And there seems to be quite an ambivalence among men as regards the outrage expressed by such authors about this issue. I like Warren Farrell's interpretation of this ambivalence. In his radical book *The Myth of Male Power* Farrell explains:

> I am often asked why men don't get as worked up as they might about women — particularly poor women — having to use their bodies as prostitutes. Because most men unconsciously experience themselves as prostitutes every day — the miner, the fire-fighter, the construction worker, the logger, the soldier, the meat-packer — these men are prostitutes in the direct sense, they sacrifice their bodies for money and for their families. The middle-class man is a prostitute of a different sort: he recalls that when his children were born, he gave up his dreams of becoming a novelist and began the nightmare of writing ad copy for a product he didn't believe in — something he would have to do every workday for the rest of his life. The poorer the man, the more he feels this. To men prostitution is not a female-only occupation. Most men barely allow themselves to think about the freedom to look within themselves until after their families are as economically secure as they desire. But many a man finds that just as his goal is within reach, his family is wishing for a nicer home, a better car, a private college. If he is one of the rare men able to satisfy his family enough to look within, he fears discovering the prostitute he has become in the process of providing for others.

It is perhaps useful to comment here that in all these discussions about the ways that men relate badly to women there is a flip side worth consideration. Women do not hold the patent on suffering, oppression or any other form of human anguish. Here, however, we wish to look more closely at ways that men objectify women.

Objectifying women can take many forms. Well-known examples are those of the trophy wife and the surrogate mother. The trophy wife is a symptom of some men's egotistical competition with other men. His relationship with a woman is just one part of a programme of self-aggrandisement. Once again he falls prey to the conditioning of his formation and sees that his value as a man is increased if he is seen to capture a beautiful woman. And in most of these cases capture is the appropriate description. The value is on the physical appearance of the woman. She is his possession, to be displayed to other males at social occasions. If she is sexually adept then all the better for he can make reference to this in male company. The man who pursues this form of relationship is not interested in intimacy, in the challenge of getting to truly know his partner, she is simply an appendage, and as long as she does not challenge him or look for more than he is prepared to give then the situation works. Much can be said of the woman who lets herself be used in this way but that is not the central concern of this present discussion.

The surrogate mother is another form of objectifying women. This is a relationship whereby a man uses a woman to cater for his needs as his mother did, with little or no interest in the welfare or development of the woman. The old description of 'taking a wife' has a resonance in this regard. The woman in this situation repeats her own modelling after her mother and derives her self-esteem and sense of identity from how well she looks after her man. In some ways this kind of relationship manages to avoid the complexity of an adult intimacy. The man behaves as a child and thus avoids the pain and difficulty of learning to relate as an adult to his spouse. The woman acts as parent and also avoids the task of self-knowledge and self-expression. In a historical context where there was little priority, time or energy left for the pleasures of communication, this form of relationship was probably quite functional. The man's physical health was in most cases an essential element of the security of the family. His role was to work hard, usually in physically demanding environments, running the risk of injury or disease, and provide the wherewithal for his spouse and children to eat and dress and be warm. Thus it was in everybody's best interest to keep the man as rested and healthy as possible. In the modern world where a major shift has occurred in the focus of relationships this type of objectification is unhealthy for all concerned.

Women as sex objects

When we speak of objectifying women most people immediately think of men using women as sex objects. This is a broader issue than that of prostitution, which is discussed above. In some feminist writing there is a tendency to suggest that male sexual orientation towards women is in all cases a form of objectification. Feminist author Luce Irigaray is typical of this kind of thinking. She writes in 'This sex which is not one':

> Woman, in this sexual imaginary, is only a more or less obliging prop for the enactment of man's fantasies. That she may find pleasure there in that role, by proxy, is possible, even certain. But such pleasure is above all a masochistic prostitution of her body to a desire that is not her own, and it leaves her in a familiar state of dependency upon man. Not knowing what she wants, ready for anything, even asking for more, so long as he will 'take' her as his 'object' when he seeks his own pleasure. Thus she will not say what she herself wants; moreover she does not know or no longer knows what she wants . . . Woman's desire would not be expected to speak the same language as man's; woman's desire has doubtless been submerged by the logic that has dominated the west since the time of the Greeks. Within this logic, the predominance of the visual,

> and of discrimination and individualisation of form, is particularly foreign to female eroticism.

Perhaps the issues of visual cues and focus on shape and form are foreign to female sexual response (although I'm not thoroughly convinced of this myself, I acknowledge the superior knowledge of women writers in this regard). Visual cues are, however, central to the male's sexual attraction to the female. There seems, therefore, to be some confusion in some of what Irigaray and others write in separating out what is normal and healthy male sexual attraction and what is abusive objectification. This issue can be approached in the manner of two questions. Is it possible for a man to be sexually attracted to a woman without seeing the body of a woman as a focus of his desire? And is this part of his sexual response by definition abusive? I think not in both instances.

Enormous scientific evidence suggests that visual cues are an important part of sexual response for males. Furthermore there is a body of evidence to suggest that, in terms of physical survival, certain visual cues for engaging a mate are clearly important. In Roman times women who were well fed and rotund were the object of male desire. Simply put, this attractiveness is based on the fact that in those times to be robust meant physical health. (The fastest athletes and the toughest warriors were the male equivalents in the stakes of sexual attraction.) Nowadays a more symmetrical form is attractive because it suggests physical health and fitness. It is rather silly to equate the visual attractiveness of women in the sexual drama of attraction and seduction to some form of objectification. It's simply a biological and natural sexual response. When we stroll beside a bakery and get the savoury smell of freshly baked bread we naturally salivate, when we see something that we fear we tense our muscles, when we view a scene of beauty our pupils dilate.

When men see the female form they are stimulated into a

sexual interest and evaluation. Science has now calculated just how curvy a woman has to be to inspire immediate sexual attraction — the waist must measure no more than 60 to 70 per cent of the hip circumference. According to evolutionary psychologist Gangestad, 'The literature shows that women with a 0.7 waist-hip ratio have a sex typical hormone profile in the relationship of oestrogen to testosterone . . . It appears that males have evolved to pay attention to this cue that ancestrally was related to fertility.' On the other side of the coin women are attracted to men who are symmetrical, but interestingly the power of this attraction changes over the period of the menstrual cycle; at time of ovulation the attraction to physical symmetry is at its highest. These and a plethora of scientific findings concerning sexual attraction tell us that the human sexual response is thus as natural and as definite as those of salivating to the smell of fresh bread and dilation of the pupils in response to pleasure. These responses are morally neutral. What is at issue, of course, is how men proceed consequent to this immediate response. Just because we salivate at the smell of the fresh bread does not mean we can rob the bakery. So what then is sexual objectification?

Some men treat women simply as sex objects for use for sexual gratification. Others use women as sex objects to sell products. The use of male sexual response as a way to market products, sometimes the product itself being sexual gratification (pornography, prostitution, sex-related entertainment), and to make money is a widespread phenomenon that requires brief note in the present discussion. In a consumer-oriented market economy most things that are sacred are denigrated by being turned into methods to catch the eye or ear of the consumer. Some recent examples come to mind, where things that are sacred to most men are turned into tricks for selling products. The Native American ritual of preparing the tribal chief for his death is one case in point. As he is laid down in his final place of rest, a hauntingly beautiful scenic location, the chief tells his son that 'today is a good day to die' (a traditional phrase in Native American lore). This scene is turned upside down as he discovers a particular brand of chocolate bar in his son's pocket. Another example opens with the scene of an ageing man reminiscing on his failure to prove himself a warrior. After raiding the eagle's nest, taming the feral stallion, climbing the most difficult rock face, he fails at the final challenge, a special way of spinning a particular brand of beer bottle. And again, a young man daydreams of saving the life of a young girl, throwing himself in front of the speeding truck and whisking this beautiful girl away from impending doom to the music of 'You've got to search for the hero inside yourself'. The daydream ends with the punchline that a particular car is as individual as you are. All these and others use what is known about the male psyche to sell products.

Marketing uses everything that is known about us to sell us something, and the most time-honoured practice is to use men's visual response to the female form to get their money. There are as many examples that use what is known of female desires and biases in this manner — from the lady who loves one particular brand of chocolates to the young, well-honed man drinking a soft drink being ogled by an audience of young women in the multistorey office building where he cleans windows. These are not a simple matter of sexism, they are examples of the prostitution of all that is sacred to the great god of Mammon.

In the present context when we talk of men objectifying women we are referring to this as sexual objectification, which is a narrower meaning of the term. Objectification in this situation is a dysfunctional relationship which is limited to the man using the woman as an object of sexual gratification. There seem to be at least two elements at work in relationships marked out by this way of behaving.

Psychological immaturity and sexual addiction

In the first instance we can see that certain men are unable to form a meaningful relationship with a woman. This means that all the different facets of relating — communication, friendship, respect, compatibility, affection and love — are absent. The relationship is simply a biological function that provides sexual release and pleasure. Men who are damaged in their ability to form deep relationships may simply see women as objects of sexual use. These men are more likely to use pornography as a means of self-titillation and to confine themselves to short-term encounters that create no emotional bond. I heard an interview recently with male actors in what is now rather euphemistically called adult film. I reflected on the notion of pornography being termed adult film and thought that the term is rather misplaced. Such films are actually adolescent if that is not being too harsh on adolescents, many of whom are romantic and idealistic.

Men who use women as sex objects are in some cases emotionally retarded. They have not grown beyond the stage of genitality into mature sexuality, and their focus is on copulation rather than intimacy. Anne Dickson is again insightful in understanding some of the dynamics of such men. Discussing male sexual problems she says:

> It is hardly surprising that most information about men's sexual problems centres around the penis: either he cannot get an erection or his erection isn't hard enough or he comes too quickly or finds it difficult to come at all. Once again the culture equates a man's sexuality solely with the function of his penis. Certainly his penis is important, but the problem lies in the fact that the line between the penis and the heart has been broken. Since the penis has become detached from the heart, sex has become detached from care — both care of self and care of others.

Another issue related to the sexual objectification of women is that of sexual addiction. I believe that there has been some distortion in what people think of male sexuality as a result of ignorance of the phenomenon of sexual addiction. There is a parallel here to the history of alcoholism. For centuries people who became addicted to alcohol were harshly judged and condemned for their abuse of this substance with all the concomitant problems that it brings in its wake — violence, sickness, unreliability and chaos. In recent decades millions of people who suffer this disorder have been able, through advances in its treatment, to find recovery and to live lives enhanced and healed. Most of these would have wasted away, continuing down an inexorable path of destruction, without getting the help that is now available.

Sexual addiction is a real problem that affects some people. Sex addicts (both male and female) are the objectifiers par excellence. Like most addictions, sexual addiction has certain defining qualities. In an earlier book, *Addiction: The CommonSense Approach*, I give the following summary that is of relevance here:

> Sex addicts are compulsively engaged in the use of sexual experience for emotional distraction and relief. Their sexual behaviour has little to do with intimacy or relationship. Nor has it anything to do with the relatively normal sexual needs that some people express by having a number of sexual partners, particularly during their early adulthood. Rather sex addiction is a compulsively driven need to use sex to relieve that addict's inner sense of emptiness, or to alleviate anxiety or distress.

Modern society offers the sex addict an almost inexhaustible supply of sex-related stimulation. Sex toys, pornography and sex guides can all be used to intensify the creation of sexual excitement. By tuning out of reality by consistently using fantasy and masturbation, drinking in the pictures and the stimulation, the sex addict gradually erodes any semblance of normal sexuality (which for most includes a certain level of fantasy and masturbation). In sexual addiction the ability to experience true sexual love is corrupted. Sex addicts confuse the biochemical sensations of sexual stimulation for the spiritual connection involved in sexual love. As the feelings of emptiness increase, the person tries harder to fill it with what is actually causing the emptiness, leading to the futile cycle that seems to be a central part of all addictions, namely using something to meets one's needs that cannot do so and that damages the person in the process.

From what is known thus far about addiction, males outnumber females in almost all the major addictions. I believe this is in no small part a result of the damage to men's emotional development that occurs in childhood. The need to alter mood, to relieve emotional pain and to create emotional sensations is more intense in men because they have so few healthy avenues to experience themselves emotionally. Sex addiction from its mild to most severe form is more prevalent among men and because, heretofore, it was not seen as an emotional/spiritual disorder, it has been used to further some biased notions about normal male sexual behaviour towards women. Male sex addicts objectify women, male alcoholics are more likely to be violent towards women, male drug pushers are more likely to become pimps and so on. Certain types of disordered men objectify and abuse women. Sexual objectification of women by men has nothing to do with normal healthy male sexuality.

(iv) Submission

A fourth type of dysfunctional relationship is one where the male lives and operates in the relationship from a position of submission. He can be seen as the traditional hen-pecked husband, or again the — quiet as a mouse — decent man who does whatever his spouse wishes. Usually, this relationship is characterised by complete lack of respect for the male on the part of the female. She tends to make sarcastic remarks about him to others, and berates him and criticises him at every turn.

Inevitably, the man in this situation becomes depressed and withdrawn, thus further convincing his partner that he is a wimp. Being a man in this situation means also that he is very unlikely to be able to get the help he needs to cope with this problem.

Some of these relationships are also characterised by physical violence towards the man. In a recent documentary on this topic I listened with keen interest to men describing their sense of futility and shame that they were being beaten by their partners. They all described the difficulty they encountered in telling anyone of the problem because they were convinced no one would believe that a grown man, who in most cases is physically more powerful, could let himself be beaten by a woman. Most men of course can understand how this can happen. The conditioning that one does not hit a woman is very deep indeed and those men who beat women are in the minority and are rejected by other men. We have seen earlier that the fellowship of men has certain unspoken rules, one being that we should protect women, and those who hurt women are seen as scum.

The dynamics of this kind of relationship are worthy of note. I don't believe that this kind of dysfunctional relationship is simply a reversal of the oppressive one. The submissive man comes into a relationship with a different psychological profile than does the woman in the oppressed relationship. And, in my opinion, the woman who dominates him and ridicules him is, in general, not operating out of fear. I am reluctant to discuss the reasons and dynamics of the female in this role, leaving that to a female author who can perhaps have a more accurate understanding of a woman who needs to damage and de-self a man. I can, however, make some comment on the man who becomes de-selfed through relating to women in this way.

Submission and male fear

In general, men who enter such a relationship have a deeply felt fear of women and a lack of confidence in themselves. Their fear of the feminine is not unlike that discussed earlier in the context of oppression. The man in this situation, however, does not react to his fear by trying to dominate, intimidate and de-self the woman, rather he tries his best to please her and to avoid her anger. This for some women is a source of anger and frustration and as a consequence she loses her respect for him. Sensing her disapproval, the man continues to try to become what she wants to the point where he loses any sense of his own self. He becomes emasculated in the relationship, often repeating some form of earlier emasculation in his relationship with his mother. The process of de-selfing described above in the context of oppression is repeated except here it is the man who is the victim.

One useful key as to why such men allow themselves to be hurt in this way lies in the man's sense of confidence in his own masculinity. At some stage a man in this situation has failed to develop what can be called his independent masculine energy and has instead tried to define himself by way of pleasing a woman. He may also tend towards idealising the female as described above. I recently had a discussion with a very kind and gentle soul of a man about this issue. He had suffered greatly in his relationship with his wife, who eventually left him. In the leaving she made full use of his gentle nature and his desire to please her by destroying him financially. After some years of trying to pull himself together and rebuild his life he had again embarked on the task of finding a soulmate.

As we discussed this issue it became clear to me that he was once again heading into a dangerous territory. His efforts to meet someone worthy of his soulful and sensitive nature seemed to me to be almost wholly concerned with trying to prove to a woman that he was an attractive and gentle man who would bring many riches of intellect and emotion to a relationship. He seemed chagrined to find that this approach was not successful. I suggested that it needed to change. I believe that, in general, women are perceptive and curious and that he need have little doubt that his attractive qualities would be clearly seen by women with whom he came in contact. If, however, he tried to prove them this would suggest that he lacked sufficient confidence and independence, qualities that for many women are attractive in a man. And furthermore, he may become prey to someone who sees his vulnerability and uses it for her own purpose. He may find himself once again with someone who abuses his gentle nature because he was too focused on pleasing her to be able to accurately evaluate her character. And this brings us to the topic of masculine energy.

Evelyn Bassoff's engaging book *Between Mothers and Sons* offers some useful clarity on this matter. She cites John Welwood's *Journey of the Heart* where he uses Chinese philosophy as a way of framing the difference between male and female energy. Masculine energy is the yang — the principle of centrifugal force that separates and pulls away, and the yin or female energy is the principle of centripetal force that draws in and connects. Like thunder and lightning, yang pierces, penetrates and arouses; like the life-giving earth with its rivers and streams, yin energy nurtures, accommodates and flows. Both sexes have yin and yang energy but according to Welwood males have a larger proportion of yang energy and could be said to 'belong to the yang', females have a larger proportion of yin energy and could be said to belong to the yin. Using this model we can say that my friend was approaching his task of finding a soulmate by relying on his yin energy rather than living his life through his yang energy and letting himself trust that the feminine would be attracted to it.

In relationships where men live in submission to women it is usually because they cannot access or operate from their masculine energy. Bassoff defines this thus: 'Healthy male energy has everything to do with being effective and engaged in life; it is focus, determination and perseverance. The samurai call this vital energy ki, ki power causes a man to leap into the battle of life rather than to take a passive stance vis-à-vis life's tasks and struggles.' Some men, as we have seen earlier, experience life through an emasculated ego. In doing so they seek security and passivity in relationships with women. A proportion of these are relatively successful in doing so because they choose a woman who is satisfied to relate as surrogate mother. Others, however, find themselves overwhelmed because they choose a partner who either is embittered to begin with or develops her anger and frustration along the way, contributed to, in no small part, by the sense of her man being, to her mind, useless.

Summary

This chapter has examined some of the more prevalent forms of dysfunctional relationships where men are concerned. After reading it you may ask, are there no healthy relationships between men and women? I believe that healthy adult relationships between men and women are those that nourish and enhance both partners' lives, and furthermore I believe that they are relatively rare. (I have described elements of such relationships in some detail in *Healing Life's Hurts*.) Most men have to rely on a process of trial and error to learn about intimacy, healthy communication and contented companionship with women. For some this process works and they undo some of the obstacles that go with their formation and eventually find the rich prize of intimacy. For others the hit-and-miss effort of building such relationships is too difficult, costs too much, or despite their best efforts is unsuccessful, often leaving men bereft and inadequate in the realm of intimate love.

8 Inadequate Skills for Fatherhood

Introduction

The subject of fatherhood is a vast terrain and can only be briefly explored in the present context. The main thrust of my argument in this chapter is that the seeds of a man's role as father are sown in the relationship with his own father. And that in current Western society we are bereft of good father models. Fatherhood requires skill, ingenuity, wisdom, humour and most of all an active interest in the development of children. These are learned as boys grow into manhood by way of their own fathers' interest in them and the influence of significant men, uncles, grandads, teachers and mentors. When we examine the qualities that men have brought to their understanding and treatment of children we are looking at an arid landscape indeed. Reflecting on my own experience with my father, as well as many therapeutic conversations of men in my generation talking about their dads, several themes emerge that seem to pose difficulty for men as they carry out the fathering role. In general, fathers are characterised as, at best, benign but emotionally distant, preoccupied, ignorant of children's needs and uncommunicative. At worst they are seen as brutal, toxic and destructive.

Emotional distance

Emotional distance does not mean that a father is not loving, proud and excited by his children. It means that he cannot relate these feelings in his relationship with them. An example from my own life nicely illustrates this.

Recently, I sat at table with Owen, my dear friend for twenty years, my twelve-year-old daughter, Sarah, and my fifteen-year-old son, David. It had been a year since Owen's last visit and I was looking forward to his seeing my children again. I prepared a nice meal and we sat and talked. My children are fascinated by our relationship, by the obvious differences between us and by the warmth and affection we share and show for each other. During the discussion Sarah asked me if her grandfather had been a good father to me. I spoke about him for some time and I felt a deep movement happening in the room. Owen lost his father to cancer when he was in his late teens and so had never had an adult relationship with his dad. David and I are in that magical and sometimes harrowing stage of father-son struggle as he asserts his need to be counted as a man rather than a boy, and his need to do battle with me as part of his rite of passage. But for those moments something rare and beautiful happened. I recounted a story to the company that for me summed up so much of my relationship with Dad.

My father and mother married in the fifties and had six children under the age of seven (no twins) by the early sixties. Rachel, my youngest sister, arrived as a surprise bundle some years later. My father stopped working for the national transport company in 1963 in order to set up his own business. I was six years old and had five siblings. My childhood was marked out by an awareness of just how hard my parents worked and how much they suffered. I did not understand their ideals of establishing some financial security and creating something that could be handed down to the next generation. These goals exhausted them and deflected them from some of the key elements involved in helping children form secure and healthy personalities. When parents suffer, their children do also and we had a difficult and sometimes traumatic childhood. In hindsight, I cannot fathom how they managed as well as they did.

I bonded with my father early in life and remember a constant curiosity about him. He was absolutely impossible to fathom. He never spoke of feelings. The only time I saw him cry was a small tear in his eye at his mother's deathbed. He lived for his work and never stopped worrying. One of the great privileges for me now is to see him content in old age, as he regularly counsels me not to worry about things. I have to smile to myself when I hear this. Financial insecurity dogged the family, business ebbed and flowed, and with each change of season new concerns emerged. My mother's emotional and physical health broke under the strain of so much work and worry. The story I told that night summarises for me all that was and is good about my father as well as reflecting his inability to save me from carrying some of the pain and struggle of his life into mine.

I was ten years old. It was a Saturday in our second shop, purchased when things looked good and the possibility for expansion seemed a good idea. Market forces changed soon after and the business went into decline. That Saturday, for some unknown reason (prayer perhaps, I'm sure my parents prayed hard for survival), the shop was extremely busy. The market was on in town and country people flocked to it. We were busy selling and fixing and I remember the constant focused attention I gave to spending my all for the work in hand. (Ironically, my children always comment now at the intensity that surrounds me when I am focused on a project — they have had to grow not to fear it.) As that evening wore on I remember at one stage my father stopping at the door of the workshop watching me; I had made a mistake in one of the repair jobs and he helped me to rectify it. If my memory serves me, some positive comment was made about me by an old man who was waiting for the repair. Closing time came, I was physically exhausted but bright and felt good, a feeling of having done a good job. My father stood at the counter adding up the takings for the day. I was polishing some article for the display when he came over to me, looked at me with a very special expression and handed me a pound note. I will never forget the feeling. This was so much more than a father handing money to his child — something I have plenty of experience of! Nothing was said, but in some awesome and primal way I knew that I had graduated into the world of men. He communicated in his own silent way that he was proud of me. That for me was the meaning of that pound and I have never earned one as precious since, nor will I ever.

Twenty-five years later Dad and I had built a communicative relationship. We went regularly for a drink and a chat together. One such evening, in the midst of all kinds of conversation, I told him of my memory of that day, and he surprised me by saying that he himself had never forgotten it. It was very special for him too. In all the intervening years, marked out by my distress with my parents for their inadequacies, in the struggles encountered in my own life that I could not share with them, and in the important task of healing the wounds from my own past, it still stands out as a beacon. To some that may seem tragic — surely childhood should be replete with memories of being cherished and praised. Yes it should, but for most men of my generation, to be able to recount one deep moment of connection with their father is the exception.

And so I told the company that night that my father was a good man, a gentle soul, a deep, creative and resolutely independent figure, who, like most men of his time, knew little about raising children. I looked at my own son's reaction when I told them that I worked very hard throughout my late teens and early adult life to teach my father how to speak openly to me. And that I had my first real conversation with my father when I was twenty-five years old. I have subsequently had many such conversations because since he mastered the art of starting a sentence with the words 'I think' or 'I feel' and lost the need to be completely in control and managing the whole world he has been able to express the beauty that lies within him, and I, for my part, have been greatly blessed to watch his emergence.

My father resembles so many fathers that I've heard about. Recently, I listened to a radio programme that dealt with this topic. One of the callers who rang in was a sixty-year-old man. His voice broke as he talked of the great grief he felt about his dad. He knew he was loved by his father but could never remember any overt expression of that love. In my work I consistently encounter men in their forties and fifties who are striving to gain that magical potion of a father's expression of pride and love. Pride in this context means that the son has proved adequate to the definition of success that his father believes in. Yes, it is almost always based on achievement of some kind or other. Perhaps the role of fatherhood throughout the aeons has been to drive civilisation forward as the males seek to prove their worth in a way that females rarely have need to do. By withholding praise and affection most fathers make their sons insecure and driven. Others just give up in despair. Perhaps emotional distance has some evolutionary significance. That for me and most men is, however, cold comfort, and it is a practice we must shed if we are to raise our own sons into confident men.

Preoccupation

Closely related to emotional distance is preoccupation. We have seen above that boys are taught early to define themselves by what they do, rather than by the nature of their relationships. This conditioning has a twofold impact that becomes particularly problematic when men become fathers. Firstly, relationships become secondary to activity. Secondly, this emphasis on doing encourages most men to relinquish the inward focus that is necessary for spiritual growth and self-understanding.

The first impact means that fathers will be preoccupied with achievement, success, problem solving and worries to the detriment of being involved with their children. Many men spend the formative years of their children's lives busily working to ensure their future, and so many men find that the years of striving mean that the young man or woman that they send to college is a stranger to them. And even more painfully, these young adults, who have no idea of the meaning of the sacrifice that put them there, reject and ridicule their fathers. This was shown with dramatic poignancy in the film *Dead Poets Society*. The young man whose dream is to be an actor is spurned by his father, who cannot change his values to incorporate his son's aspirations. He cannot make this change because he has spent his whole life sacrificing himself for his son's well-being. To be able to value the son's aspiration is to make a mockery of his own sacrifice and to encourage his son to become something he believes is bad for him. Additionally, he has neither the communication nor the connection with his son to be able to navigate this crisis. Although the film is somewhat biased in its sympathies and demonises the father, it effectively reveals the impasse between father and son. This impasse emerges when fathers have been too preoccupied with providing for their sons' welfare rather than relating to them and learning through the relationship to reshape and adjust to a new set of beliefs about masculinity.

Harry Chapin's song 'The Cat's in the Cradle', written in the 1970s, is perhaps the most poignant and eloquent description of preoccupation and emotional distance that I know.

> A child was born just the other day
> He came into the world in the usual way
> But there were planes to catch and bills to pay
> He learned to walk while I was away
> And he was talking 'fore I knew it and as he grew
> He said I'm going to be like you, Dad
> You know I'm going to be just like you
>
> And the cat's in the cradle and the silver spoon
> Little boy blue and the man in the moon
> When you coming home, Dad, I don't know when
> We'll get together soon, son
> You know we'll have a good time then

Well my son turned ten just the other day
He said thanks for the ball, Dad, come on let's play
You can teach me to throw, I said not today
I got a lot to do and he said OK
And he walked away his smile never dimmed
And it said I'm gonna be like him yeah
You know I'm gonna be like him

And the cat's in the cradle and the silver spoon
Little boy blue and the man in the moon
When you coming home, Dad, I don't know when
We'll get together then, son
You know we'll have a good time then

Well he came from college just the other day
So much like a man I just had to say
Son, I'm proud of you can you sit a while
He shook his head and said with a smile
What I'd really like are the keys of the car
Can I have them please

And the cat's in the cradle and the silver spoon
Little boy blue and the man in the moon
When you coming home son, I don't know when
We'll get together then, Dad
You know we'll have a good time then

Well I've long since retired and my son's moved away
I called him up just the other day
Said I'd like to see you if you don't mind
He said I'd love to, Dad, if I had the time
You see the new job's such a hassle
And the kids have the flu
Been sure nice talking to you, Dad

And as he hung up the phone
It occurred to me
He'd turned out just like me

Ignorance about children

To a large extent it is only in this generation that parents in Western society have the necessary information available to understand the complex task that is child rearing. And this information also helps us to understand that there is much at risk in the newly formed approaches to child rearing. Marie Winn writes in *Children without a Childhood*:

> At the heart of the matter lies a profound alteration in society's attitude towards children. Once parents struggled to preserve children's innocence, to keep childhood a carefree golden age, and to shelter children from life's vicissitudes. The new era operates on the belief that children must be exposed early to adult experience in order to survive in an increasingly complex and uncontrollable world. The Age of Protection has ended. An Age of Preparation has begun.

Until very recently parents had little information on the nature of children. Societies gave parents a basic set of primitive rules that were considered some way useful, but often were merely the combined ignorance of a few. 'Children should be seen and not heard,' 'Crying is a child exercising his lungs' and 'Four-hour feeds establish discipline' are a few of the more dangerous ones that informed many parents of this century. Certain societies, ones that some mistakenly call primitive, have far healthier rules for child development than we have had. Feeding on demand, lots of play, constant companionship with parents, gradual apprenticeship in the arts of hunting, tracking, building, worship and so on, led to emotional security, confidence and stability in the community.

While I am somewhat wary of Winn's notion of the era of protection — many statistics suggest that children were ill protected in the past — I agree that the whole role of childhood in modern society has changed. She argues further that 'Today's integration of children into adult life marks a curious return to that old, undifferentiated state of affairs in which childhood and adulthood were merged into one.'

If this is the age of preparation how well equipped are men for the task of fatherhood? We have seen above that the formative experiences in becoming a man have led men to become emotionally distant and preoccupied when it comes to building relationships with children. A third element, however, is of particular relevance when we consider fatherhood as part of preparing children for life. In order to do this adequately men need to know something about the nature of children. In general, they are severely limited in this area. The emphasis on doing rather than on being that is a constant theme in the lives of most men means that when a man becomes a father he is unlikely to know that quite a lot of his reactions to his children are about himself rather than the children. This is because his conditioning has directed him away from self-understanding. The focus on doing elevates the external events in the man's perception and reduces his internal awareness. Thus, his relationships with his children will lack insight into the complexity of their world. This further alienates him from them.

Summary

This chapter has examined the impact of formative experiences in men's lives on their roles as fathers. It has been argued that many men come into the task of fatherhood inadequately prepared for it. These inadequacies are a result of difficulties in their own relationship with their fathers as well as influences that affect men's ability to create emotional bonds. Three areas where men struggle as fathers were examined: emotional distance from children, preoccupation — often with the needs to provide material support for children at the cost of a communicative relationship, and thirdly, lack of knowledge of the nature of children. These areas of difficulty mean that many children lose one of the most enriching experiences in life, that of a close emotional and communicative relationship with their father, and many men equally miss out on one of life's great joys, a close emotional and communicative relationship with their children.

9 Imbalanced Men

Introduction

Thus far we have examined a series of difficulties that runs throughout the lives of men as a result of their formative experiences. Robert Bly talks of the deforming of personality as a result of these kinds of influences. He argues in *The Sibling Society* that

> Men and women were forced into specialisation of labour just to keep their clan of fifty people alive. Half of them were sick all the time; women died in childbirth; no one got enough vitamins; people were old at thirty. The list of deprivation is endless; and the specialised gender roles, adopted out of fear and need, caused deformations in the personalities of both men and women.

This chapter presents a series of what can be called deformed male personalities. Each man is a unique individual and each develops some way of dealing with the damaging influences that are part of male conditioning. Part of that way will be influenced by genetic or inborn temperament. Part will be determined by the severity of the forces that are placed on him. Some infant boys, for example, are more placid than others, some are more aggressive, some are more sensitive. The influences that shape men are presented on top of the young boy's temperament and as a result will form his unique personality. A sensitive child put under severe competitive pressure will be more damaged than one who is tougher in temperament and put under less pressure. While acknowledging that every man is an individual in his own right, certain types or general themes emerge when we look at men in general. This chapter, the last in this section, combines much of what is presented above into a series of stereotypes about men. Each of the types described below is a collage of features, none describes any man in particular but each tries to communicate in general terms the way that men of different temperamental make-up develop and behave as a way of coping and dealing with the expectations and pressures that inhere in their conditioning as men.

The strong oak

Eileen sits across from me and begins to cry. She has recently discovered that her husband of twenty years has had an affair. In the initial sessions she spoke of her surprise and shock, and was numb and detached. Now she is fifteen minutes into the consultation and she gradually gets in touch with the raw pain that will take much healing. As she describes her husband, Paul, she uses terms familiar to many men, reliable, honest, hard-working, practical and emotionally unavailable. She acknowledges that the relationship lacked passion and spontaneity. Their love had cooled into a very predictable and decent sort of lifestyle. As I probed a bit deeper she began to talk about the distance that she felt had grown between them. She talks of having given up on there being a satisfying emotional connection and an acceptance that life has some burdens for everyone and all in all she was content with Paul as a good provider and a 'strong oak'. I ask her to explain this and she talks about her picture of the oak tree. When she was young there was an oak at the corner of her road in the country and it was always a reminder to her of permanence and strength. In all the varieties of weather and season it would stand firm and unscathed. Paul to her mind was like this oak tree, lacking in some of the spontaneity she would like, a bit distant and somewhat firm with the children, but all in all a good man. It never entered her mind that he would stray from her.

It never entered Paul's mind either. As I got to know him he reflected so many of the attributes of the 'strong oak'. Such men are driven by responsibility. They take on the role of masculinity in the following way. They are generally men of strong belief in working hard and being responsible. They are firmly committed to seeing life as a problem to be solved and are critical of those who seem frivolous or lazy. Strong oak men are almost completely out of touch with their emotions. They work from the rational mind and are inclined to minimise their needs. When children come along they tend to be conservative and strict, and some have particular difficulty in coping with the struggles of adolescent children. They expect their children to behave as young adults. They are loyal and very supportive in a practical and distant sort of way. If they marry a woman who wants fun, overt emotional expression of affection, lots of communication, they can become even more distant because they are unable to cope with these demands. These men are most prone to stress-related physical diseases. Their bodies bear the brunt of the emotional repression as well as a certain neglect of their physical needs for rest, entertainment, recreation and health care. These men are likely to let physical disease progress before getting treatment, and less likely to take treatment with proper care when it is required. They have a high tolerance for pain and a dismissal of illness as a form of weakness. Strong oak men tend to believe that they are invincible and in any case they have no time to get sick or need rest.

Most 'strong oak' men are faithful to their vows. They have a high degree of self-control which they are proud of and tend to judge those who don't match up, including their spouse and children. Because they are actually emotionally imbalanced they can be blind-sided by their emotional needs. This is where such men are prone to have affairs. In general, such affairs start with meeting a seemingly 'weaker' or emotionally vulnerable woman who appeals to their strong sense of protection and strength. In denial that they are becoming emotionally and sexually entangled they continue to believe that they are fully in control and that they are just being helpful until the control that has been unconsciously weakening breaks. They then 'find themselves' in the midst of a full-blown sexual encounter. Strong oak men usually are torn apart by the ensuing guilt. Some abandon their spouse because they can find no way to live with themselves in her company. Others pick up the pieces but never really deal with the causes and live under the shadow of guilt that they try to make amends for by redoubling their efforts to be a good husband. Others just withdraw further and thereby increase the suffering of those who need and want some emotional connection.

The playboy

The playboy reacts to the demands of masculinity by developing into an escape artist, driven by a need to escape facing up to the serious aspect of life. He refuses to take on the mantle of responsibility, competition and achievement that so inheres in the cultivation of young men. He rebels against this hard and sometimes ruthless set of demands, but does so in a way that is non-aggressive. Finding very subtle strategies of avoidance, he then takes these into adulthood. Avoidance can include always having a ready excuse for not doing something and promising the earth with no intention of fulfilling the promise. The promise is made because most people tend to take others at their word. That means that the promise keeps the person happy in their trust and allows the playboy to escape. He can deal with the consequences later. This reveals another important aspect of the playboy, he lives in the moment. As long as he is happy now, he doesn't care what is around the next corner. This generally means that all kinds of problems are storing up that will eventually have to be dealt with. Of particular significance is financial difficulty. Playboys are constantly in financial trouble.

They will borrow from Peter to pay Paul. Some begin to gamble and end up as compulsive gamblers, ruining their own lives and the lives of those close to them.

Along with avoidance and living in the moment, most playboys develop an important strategy, that of charm. Charm involves making people feel good about themselves. It includes humour, compliments, teasing and a variety of other very sophisticated manipulative techniques. Charm can be sincere, used as part of a genuine desire to encourage and affirm others. In this case it is a minor part of a generally positive attitude to people. The playboy, however, uses charm as a significant tool to get him out of the trouble that occurs as a result of his failure to take responsibility. He is forgiven often because he is able to defuse the anger that is evoked in adults. There is a certain irony in the fact that strong oak fathers can find that they have raised playboy sons.

In relationships with women the playboy is great fun, attractive, exciting and entertaining. This usually has the result of attracting a lot of interest from women, most of whom believe that with the right influences, and a lot of love, the more dangerous and chaotic aspects of his character will even out. Many women have lived to rue the day they believed this. The playboy is unable to take on the task of reliability within a relationship, and more particularly the devotion, consistency and patience that is required for good fatherhood. He is prone to being unfaithful to his partner and may see most women as a challenge to his well-developed seductive tactics. The playboy is damaged at a deep level in his relationship to his masculinity. He is imbalanced and this is not a simple matter of changing his behaviour. And unfortunately, most will not receive the help they need to heal the hurt and sense of impoverishment that lies underneath their entertaining but ultimately hollow lives.

The dreamer

The dreamer is a sensitive boy that is generally traumatised by the cruelty implicit in a lot of what goes as 'making a man out of him'. He is often rejected by his father because he is so sensitive. His temperament attracts him towards beauty, music, colour and generally a strong relationship with his mother. In some instances he becomes a surrogate husband, having long chats with her and unconsciously meeting many of her emotional needs for connection and communication. She is often unaware that this bond crosses the line of mother-child relationship into something else and this does untold damage to the young man that emerges out of this relationship.

The dreamer develops into adulthood with difficulties in the areas that are important elements of male energy. He cannot develop these because they are part of a traumatising system and as a result loses out on getting the healthy parts of male development. These include endurance, perseverance, focus, delaying gratification and discipline. The dreamer then cannot build a step-by-step foundation for his career. He may be very intelligent with a keen mind and a sophisticated intuition, but he generally underachieves, either because he cannot persevere with his education, or because he is rejected by the world of men since they dislike his sensitivity. If he is very talented he can sometimes survive well because he can channel his talent into some artistic endeavour such as poetry, music or art.

The dreamer is often a very tormented individual. His inner world is full of conflict, and because he is able to feel his feelings he can experience great swings of mood from elation to deep anguish. Part of these swings often include aggressive outbursts. His masculine energy is not properly integrated and his sense of rage against the world can explode onto those close to him. This seething anger is often not initially apparent when people get to meet the dreamer.

He is very prone to drug addiction, mainly as a strategy to relieve much of his pain. Dreamers who have been unable to integrate their masculine energy suffer tremendous feelings of shame and guilt that often haunt them for life. Their sensitivity and complex emotional expression, as well as their talents, are very attractive to certain kinds of women. They tend to generate a 'please love me and protect me' request to women who grow to believe that with enough tender loving care this haunted and anguished man will be healed. It doesn't work. The dreamer's problem does not lie in a lack of feminine love, it lies in the rejection and pain around his sense of being a man. Healing happens when he rebuilds the foundation of his manhood and this usually requires the love, respect and support of other men.

Little boy lost

Little boy lost is afraid. He copes with the failures and rejections of boyhood by seeking to disappear from view. As an adult he is reluctant to express himself in the world. He seeks to please others and to find a secure place where he can live out his life unnoticed. He fears change and unfamiliarity. He makes a very reliable if somewhat predictable colleague, partner and father. He is inclined to work in situations that demand little by way of creativity and spontaneity. He may be very talented and intelligent but this will rarely show because he puts security first. He feels more comfortable working with things, numbers, paper rather than working with people. Because security and predictability are so important to him, he is inclined to be very controlling and meticulous. As long as all the Is are dotted and Ts are crossed then he feels safer in the world.

His family relationships are generally marked out by a lack of passion, a dependable if somewhat boring lifestyle. He is more likely to be the submissive partner in his marriage. His fear of self-assertion leads him to want someone else to take the lead. If his partner is sympathetic to him and loves him despite his flawed emotional self then he will be content and loyal to a fault. If on the other hand she despises his fear and weakness then he is in for chronic low-level misery out of which he cannot escape. His children will benefit from his secure presence while young but grow to disrespect him as they move into adolescence. He is unable to cope with their growing anger and disrespect as well as their adolescent turmoil, and is therefore likely to become even more withdrawn. Later in life men whose fathers operate out of this distorted masculinity have much regret and often pity for him.

Recently, I had a conversation with a client whose father typified this kind of male. He spoke to me of his experience growing up. His father was a silent presence, often depressed, helpful when asked but seemingly uninterested in anything except doing his job well and keeping out of the way. As a civil servant he was respected by his colleagues and was rewarded with several promotions, none of which seemed to enliven his spirit. An insightful moment for this client occurred as he prepared to visit his father who was now ill and aged. He wished to buy him a gift, and could think of nothing that would interest him. On reflection he realised that his father was bought the same gift year in year out by all members of the family — cheap shirts. Further exploring this issue he realised that these were the only gifts that his mother would not complain about. This time the client broke the rules and bought him an expensive designer shirt. He wept as he thought of his father, who secretly liked a bit of style but never indulged his desires. On receiving this gift his father looked at his adult son of forty years with a knowing look that said I'm glad you understand. He was unable to fight for himself and had lived a life in the shadows, and his son by giving this gift in some symbolic way was saying, I am on your side, I understand what has happened to you, and I value you.

When I think of the little boy lost I am reminded of that hilarious character Henry Wilt in the humorous Tom Sharpe novels. Wilt spends his recreation from a dead-end job teaching unreceptive students at an insignificant polytechnic by taking walks along the river bank with his dog. Beaten by life and terrified of his rather aggressive and overpowering wife, he fantasises about how to kill her. Sharpe's novels are zany and over the top but do capture the futility and helplessness that inheres in the adult 'little boy lost' male.

The autocrat

The converse of the little boy lost is the autocrat. He operates his masculinity on a craving for power and he defines himself in terms of his superiority over others. He can disguise his addiction to power beneath a veil of manipulation and what can appear as diplomacy, or he can carry his need for power around with a swagger and a superior attitude. He is fiercely competitive and must reach the highest rung of the ladder in whatever role in life he chooses. He has taken the male conditioning of achievement and success to its limit and lost the perspective and balance required to carve out relationships based on respect and equality. Things must go his way or not at all. In general, his family life is deeply unhappy. His partner is de-selfed and his children live in fear. Those that rebel are rejected and criticised, those that comply lose their individuality and self-worth. This form of dysfunctional manhood is less common nowadays as educational progress and the feminist movement have raised the consciousness of the present generation. Autocrats were far more in vogue when they had the support of both political and religious institutions.

Autocratic fathers did untold damage to their children and were encouraged in doing so by these institutions that were in themselves autocratic hierarchies. Autocrats treat everyone in terms of where they are on the rungs of power. Those who are superior are envied and tacitly respected, those of inferior status are treated with derision. Most people in the modern generation have scant regard for these people. I believe that the level of rebellion and disrespect for authority that is growing at an alarming rate among young people has more to do with a rejection of autocracy than a failure to realise that some people are more knowledgeable and wiser than oneself. Autocrats give authority a bad name.

Autocrats are found in every walk of life but gravitate towards work where they will have control over people, as well as the rewards of social status. Thus, they can be found in greater proportions in the church, in the legal profession, in medicine and in politics. Of course there are many men attracted to these professions out of different motives, altruism, idealism, a desire to care and heal and so on. It becomes readily apparent, however, which of these motive forces is at work when one is in a face-to-face interaction with a man in this position. The autocrat has scant regard for other people's needs and feelings, his fulfilment comes from his sense of power over others. They are, in general, chauvinistic and racist. These aspects are grounded in their sense of power. Because they evaluate all interactions in terms of power, they see women as less powerful, tend to hold on to sexist ideas. They extend their attitudes to women to others who may be disenfranchised; the poor, the homeless, the less educated are all seen as inferior by virtue of their disempowerment. In political life they would be seen as representing the hard line on most issues. They can resort to violence as a means of wielding power. Autocratic violence is, however, different from other forms of male violence. Above we have seen in discussing the dreamer that violence that can erupt as a result of unhealed hurt and the pain of rejection. In another context below, I will discuss violence as a form of self-expression. Here, however, the violence being discussed is calculated and purposeful. It fits with what researchers call instrumental aggression. The main purpose behind such violence is to get compliance. Because violence is rarely accepted in society as a way of relating, the autocrat may reserve such behaviour for his immediate family, and only then when other forms of wielding power, verbal abuse, mental torture, neglect and so on, do not work.

Historically, autocratic men provided enormous fuel to the fires of social reformists, and tended, because they were often influential and had public exposure, to add much to the mythology of male domination and cruelty. Autocrats are simply one type of dysfunctional male. They are not representative of men in general.

The thug

The thug is driven by violence. He is representative of a growing number of disenfranchised and angry young men. His appearance as a type of distorted masculinity is strongly related to the growth of urban sprawl and the economic realities that leave many unemployed and uneducated. It may seem politically insensitive to describe certain people as thugs, and yet there seems to me little virtue in ascribing qualities to these men that they don't have. Most are fed on a steady diet of violence through thousands of hours of television and video that elevates male violence and aggression as being in some way virtuous. Their capacity for abstract thinking is diminished by a lack of stimulation, usually a violent and repressive father if he exists at all, and a gradual turning to the gang of similarly impoverished males in which to form their identity.

Evelyn Bassoff provides perceptive comments about this kind of male. She writes in *Between Mothers and Sons*:

> Crazy male energy has everything to do with violence and domination. Unfortunately we do not have to look any further than the daily newspaper, with its depressing stories of gun-toting fourth graders and twelve-year-old rapists, for examples of crazy male energy . . . The boy or man who is violently aggressive is neither a normal nor a typical male. He may be neurologically impaired; or he may have been badly abused, humiliated, exploited, neglected or exposed to scenes of domestic violence, having learned hurting as a way of life from his parents and other family members, from the popular media, or from the mean streets and schools, he perpetuates the cycle of violence.

Quentin Tarantino captures the nature of this sort of violation in his films. He provides a superb example of the absence of conscience that seems to inhere in this kind of way of being men. In *Pulp Fiction* we see a young man have his head shot off in the back of a car. Two characters, played brilliantly by John Travolta and Samuel L. Jackson, are faced with the difficulty of both cleaning the car and disposing of the body. The manner in which they approach this dilemma is amusing and informative. Not once is there a trace of any significance to the young man's death. This attitude to violent death is a theme throughout the film. Of course, a great number of films kill off characters as part of a plot, the difference in Tarantino's work is that it does it with characters that have become intimate to the audience, and the deaths seem irrelevant to the plot. Travolta's character, for example, is killed off when this is least expected. The theme of his work seems to me to underline the meaninglessness of life that leaves his characters completely unmoved by either killing or being killed. I think of Bob Dylan's poetic lines in this regard, 'when you ain't got nothing, you've got nothing to lose'.

Thugs are men who have nothing to lose. They just don't care, but their anger is not a measure of their indignity, rather it is a brutish and diminished form of being human. For some it takes on an added and even more dangerous form when it becomes connected to some ideological cant. Such ideologies from white supremacy to neo-Nazism are a fertile breeding ground for such violent men. Their violence, with or without an ideological veneer, seems to me to be a form of self-affirmation. Three hundred and fifty years ago the great philosopher Descartes, in his attempt to understand the nature of human existence, said, 'I think, therefore I am.' In the year 2000 the thug says, 'I violate, therefore I am.'

Summary

In this chapter I have explored some typical constellations of characters that reflect the way that men respond to their conditioning. The descriptions are somewhat extreme and are really only a guide towards understanding ourselves. Few men fully fit the descriptions above, but most carry some elements of one or two characterisations. The main point in the discussion is to underline that there is no one way to be a man, and there is a variety of ways men cope with and integrate the definition of manhood that has conditioned them into their character. As a consequence we have to be careful how we approach healing and growth for men. Different directions towards healing are required depending on the different forms of dysfunction. This issue is explored in the next section.

PART THREE

Towards Healthy Masculinity

10 Getting Ready for Change

Introduction

Thus far we have examined some of the central issues about what makes men the way they are. I expect that most men reading this will have a fairly typical male response, that of saying, OK, so now that we know how damaged we are, what are we going to *do* about it? As in the great one-liner Walter Mondale applied to Gary Hart in his presidential campaign: 'Where's the beef?' Men are inclined to look for straightforward and practical solutions to problems and many will look to this section of the book to sort out a lot of the complex and historical dilemmas facing men. So I must begin this section with some warnings that simple solutions are not appropriate to the kinds of issues that have been raised.

I will suggest ways forward that are practicable, in the sense that they are things that can be done, rather than simply relying on that ubiquitous old Freudian cure-all — insight. The assumption that if we know we have a problem we have the means to solve it is in the present context optimistic and inaccurate. Most of the difficulties that face men are not going to go away simply because we acknowledge them. Acknowledging them is of course absolutely necessary but is only a first step. Most of these problems have been a long time in the making and for most men the solutions take time, energy and some education into different ways of being in the world.

Before explaining the process of fundamental change, two

popular approaches to understanding and helping men need some comment. These are stress management and the mid-life crisis.

Stress management

Stress management as a concept began to take hold in the corporate structures in the 1960s. Stress became the disease of corporate man, a disease that caused him misery and endangered his health. Stress became an enemy because it cost the corporate sector enormous amounts of money. When executives that were essential to organisations' profitability became disabled or began dying early from stress-related diseases, systems needed to be put in place to do battle with this enemy.

Gymnasiums were incorporated into buildings, offices were redecorated in peaceful colours, health information was disseminated, human resources departments kept an eye on quality of life issues. These strategies helped a lot of men to cope with what was happening to them, gave them longer working lives and increased their productivity and efficiency. Much of the research and information garnered during this time eventually filtered down so that today we have a huge variety of stress management strategies available to anyone who has an interest. Bookshops adorn their shelves with all kinds of guidebooks — from meditation to massage, from breathing techniques to basking in visualised sunsets. Music cassettes bring us into the company of whales and dolphins and shamanic journeys get us to talk with totem animals and spirit guides. Most of these are useful, some highly valuable, and I use some of them myself personally and in my work with clients.

There is, however, one significant issue here — stress management is essentially a symptom relief approach. And I see it being used as a catch-all diagnosis that does not address the central difficulties that face many men and so prolongs the disease. If you take an aspirin for a toothache you will get relief. If, however, you keep increasing the dose and don't get the cause of the toothache dealt with, you may end up with a serious infection that is far more damaging than the initial cavity.

The reader may remember Jack, who killed himself rather than live in the shame of failing his family. Every lunchtime for months before his death Jack religiously practised the stress management techniques that his psychiatrist had taught him. He knew the deep breathing technique, the visualisations to use to ease his mind, the stretching and contracting muscular method of tension release. Jack, however, did not die from stress, he died from shame. He needed someone to help him deal with his definition of himself and with his pride. This would take more than a series of emotional gymnastics and mental aerobics.

I see stress management as somewhat akin to the field hospitals in the First World War. The minor sprains, flesh wounds and infections were treated and the young men were sent quickly back to the front to have their heads shot off, or their guts splattered all over no man's land. We have to be very careful just how far we apply the panacea of stress management to men's problems.

Mid-life crises

A second popular notion about men is that they inevitably fall into some kind of trough or chaos in mid-life, and that this is some kind of aberration to be endured for a time, treated with a bit of tolerance, a little medication perhaps, and a good dose of straight talking. I think it is as sexist to explain away the anguish that many men face in mid-adulthood in this way as it is to explain away women's concerns and struggles as a menstruation problem. Yes, many men show the signs of deep internal anguish and grave emotional struggle in mid-life, this is not a mid-life crisis, this is a life crisis that has been building up throughout the man's life. What happens when he reaches his forties is that much of the illusion that has been keeping him going begins to fall away and he begins to see through the false promises that told him he would get peace of mind, adequate love, a sense of self-worth and pride if he obeyed the rules of being a man, rules that I have described in detail in chapter 1. The male mid-life crisis is the collapse of an illusion that took his whole life to make, and it is diminishing to describe it in any other terms.

If managing the stresses encountered in trying to live out the demands of male conditioning is insufficient, and if we cannot reduce male problems as some developmental phase, what then is involved in addressing the issues raised in this book so far? One useful way of approaching this is to see it as involving making fundamental changes in the way men live their lives. The remainder of this book examines and suggests changes in all the fundamental aspects of male functioning.

Beginning the journey

Having commented on the need to avoid quick fixes, or patronising and minimalist explanations, two issues arise: where do we go from here, and what do we need for the journey? To the first I am suggesting that men need to shift their attention inward. They need to do what much of their life experience has prevented them from doing, they need to travel into the core of the self and to get to know their very souls.

In my opinion the key changes that need to happen in the lives of men will happen at a deeper and more meaningful level when they come as a result of a change in direction in men's relationship with themselves. Thus instead of beginning with the topics of improving relationships with others, becoming more skilful fathers and changing our beliefs and attitudes regarding work, I will examine the foundations of such changes, men's relationships with themselves. The first stage in promoting a healing of men's lives lies in helping men to move away from the external focus of their energies into a journey into themselves.

One particular film that nicely illustrates this turning inward is *Dances with Wolves*. The character of John Dunbar, a brave and intelligent warrior, requests to be posted way out in Indian country. When asked about this strange request he explains that he wants to see the frontier before it is gone. As the story unfolds he meets those extraordinary spiritual people, a tribe of Native Americans. He gets to know them, and as he becomes thawed of his prejudice and fear, he becomes enriched by their rituals, customs and spirituality. In one scene that moved me deeply he takes leave of his new friends and goes back to his own camp, where he builds a huge fire under the starry heavens and begins to dance around it. He has truly travelled to a new frontier, the frontier of his own soul. The journey towards a richer and healthier masculinity means travelling to the frontier within, rather than to the border of a new project.

For some men the notion of deepening self-awareness, of coming to terms with the complex and mysterious elements of one's nature, is a daunting task. To others it is irrelevant — just forget about it, go out, make more money, drink more pints and have more fun, leave the navel-gazing to others and get on with it is their guiding fiction. And then again to others there has been a 'still small voice' calling from within for a long time and it is a great relief to know that such a journey can be embarked upon at last. Whatever one's gut-level reaction to making a major life change which seeks to redress much of the contamination that damages men, this journey within begins with a decision. To go or not to go. Once undertaken it is hard to go back, or as one client said to me, as he encountered the wonder and pain of the journey, 'You can't put the toothpaste back in the tube.' Embarking on the path towards inner wholeness and self-insight is indeed an immense challenge. All the great prophets and teachers tell us it is the bedrock of an authentic life. They also tell us that navigating the shoals and rapids, the peaks and the gorges can be less daunting, less tortuous and demanding if we take certain things with us. We need to take commitment, endurance, patience, hope and trust. Let us look briefly at each.

Commitment

The central argument in this book is that men have been formed through forces acting on them since birth. These forces have produced great gifts in the male psyche as well as serious imbalances. To address these imbalances is a courageous and awesome challenge. When a man chooses to take that path of self-insight and growth he needs to make a commitment to himself to give it the time and energy required. It cannot be done for someone else's sake, for then he will lose sight of the meaning of this task. It may involve enormous change and it will certainly involve deep emotional upheaval.

For generations men have made deep commitments. They have scaled the highest mountains, sometimes dying in the effort, others have frozen to death in the arid and bleak wastelands of the North Pole. These men and so many like them brought enormous commitment and single-mindedness to their projects. Men's commitment to adventure, to discovery and exploration, and to pushing the boundaries of knowledge is a common theme in history. Less common is their commitment to their own evolution and growth as persons. And yet the interior world is often just as mysterious, as full of unknown forces, what Joseph Campbell calls 'strange jinn'. Sometimes there is fear, other times fatigue and then again excitement at all the possibilities that can come into view. All of this can happen only if the initial commitment is made, the commitment to keep going, not to turn back, to stay the pace. After commitment comes endurance.

Endurance

Any major change in life is going to bring doubts, fears and sometimes difficult decisions along the way. Some men are lazy and their laziness usually prevents them from growing up. Many men, however, appreciate the process of hard work. In any job there are men who are immediately recognised by others as having the quality of being a worker. These are the men who have developed endurance.

Endurance is a type of hard work, it means being prepared to suffer a bit, to stretch oneself that bit further, to discomfort oneself, in order to gain the rich prize. The prize in the context of this book involves a level of authenticity and spiritual depth that is indeed rare. Men who undertake this path become better fathers and lovers, and live more comfortably within themselves. And what richer prize could one ask for than to know, love and respect oneself, and to effectively love others? One such prize was attained by Raymond Carver, a brilliant American short story writer and poet, raised by parents who suffered much through the Depression years, the child of an alcoholic who became one himself, almost dead by age forty from the ravages of drink, only to turn around and find both recovery and a special love. In his own recovery, which lasted only until his early death at fifty, he wrote these beautiful lines, the coda for his last book of poetry, which he titled 'Late Fragment'.

> And did you get what
> you wanted from this life, even so?
> I did.
> And what did you want?
> To call myself beloved, to feel myself
> beloved on the earth.

Closely related to the quality of endurance is that of patience.

Patience

Not a particularly common trait in men. In general, men are inclined to need tangible results for their efforts and are less patient when things are vague and unclear. If a man is building a house he can see at the end of the day another layer or two of blocks. If he is building a computer database he can see the printout of new addresses, if writing a book he can do a word count at the day's end and muse, 'Hmm, well a bit more done today.' If, on the other hand, he is rebuilding a self, there are far less concrete and visible signs from one day to the next.

I reflected recently on the challenge of writing this chapter. I have seen many books on soul issues written by eminent and wise men and women. Some are four or five hundred pages long. Most men do not have the patience to commit that kind of time to soulfulness. The irony is that men who read such books are already converted, they are already on the journey and some of them are further along it than I.

Patience is required because the gains to health, happiness and wisdom come slowly and haltingly. But they do come. Patience is also related to expectations. Unrealistic expectations lead to frustration and sometimes to giving up. Realistic expectation for personal development and self-awareness as described in the chapters following means that the task is never ended. The path winds on ahead and there is no end. The whole point of the exercise is to enjoy the journey rather than live in frustrated hurry to get to the end. This is where hope plays its part.

Hope and trust

These two elements are deeply interconnected in the psyche. They go hand in hand as do hopelessness and distrust. Many men are quietly despairing, some are acting out the real experience that their lives lack meaning and substance. Beneath the surface, in the late-night ruminations, many men are asking 'What's the point?' They get up in the morning and do what they have been taught so well to do, push away the doubts and get on with it. I remember hearing a true story that illustrates this well. A young fighter pilot radioed back to base during the Vietnam War, as his radar confirmed that an MiG fighter had locked on to him. He could see a missile was on the way and his calls became more and more frantic. Then he heard the stern voice from the command centre tell him to 'Suck up your guts, son, and die like a marine.' Many men have that voice in their heads every day of the week.

Hope in this context is the belief that there is a better way and is, in the words of philosopher Gabriel Marcel, 'nothing but the active struggle against despair.' Every life is worthy of redemption. Every man deserves an opportunity to become a gentle, wise and fulfilled human being. Hope and trust means believing positively that staying on the track and not giving up will bear fruit. It means 'knowing' that if we are honest and hard-working in our endeavours the difficulties will be surmounted and the gifts of love, meaning and fulfilment will be there for us.

Support

Very few men can heal their wounds and redefine themselves as men without some form of support structure. And as we have seen earlier, male friendship tends to lack the kind of communication that is needed to help the labour and birth of new life that is part of this process. So once again men must do their best with the little means of support that are available. Engaging a counsellor can be a useful part of this process but he or she needs to be aware that what is being undertaken is a major reconstruction, rather than a redecoration. In this context some counselling for men's difficulties, especially that which is described in terms of stress management, is somewhat akin to rearranging the furniture on the *Titanic*. There is some specific guidance on this issue in my earlier book *Healing Life's Hurts*.

Summary

This chapter has laid out the challenge to men who wish to significantly address the difficulties they encounter. Many are a direct result of their personal history and social conditioning as men.

So it is decision time. It will take a minimum of one year to make significant changes that have consolidated and become part of one's character. There will be joy, pain, upset, difficult decisions around work, marriage, children and friendship. Each of the areas that I discuss in the remaining chapters is complex and my treatment of them is too brief to fully encompass their nature. This could be seen as a weakness of the book but by acknowledging it I am setting the limits of this work. The goal is to introduce each topic with a sufficient level of analysis to point men in the direction of change. Other books explore these issues at more length and I will perhaps explore some topics in more detail at a later date. So if you are ready for change, read on.

11 The Care of the Soul

Introduction

We have seen earlier that men are almost universally discouraged from developing an interior life. The prizes are there for those who forget about themselves and produce what is required. The accolades are given to the heroes who fight the battle well, who succeed in competition, who make and do. Few are the praises given to men who cultivate their own spiritual depth and emotional health. We live in a world that is powerfully biased against men becoming whole.

One of the tasks that men need to address is the care of the soul. Plato instructs us that 'the cure of the part should not be attempted without treatment of the whole, and also no attempt should be made to cure the body without the soul, and therefore if the head and the body are to be well you must begin by curing the mind: that is the first thing . . . for this is the great error of our day in the treatment of the human body, that physicians separate the soul from the body' (*Chronicles*, 156e). In this ancient precise instruction to approach healing as a holistic venture there is much wisdom. The next two chapters look at key elements in a holistic approach to healing the interior aspects of men's lives. This chapter is about some of the basic tasks that men can engage in to cultivate a sense-based spirituality, the one following examines the pursuit of meaning. The remaining chapters are the outworkings of these growth areas into all the key aspects of day-to-day living.

The spirituality of the senses

I have borrowed this phrase from John O'Donoghue. He is a philosopher and theologian who seems to me to capture in a very practicable manner a way to take spiritual growth out of the elite realm of dreamers and mystics (worthy and all as they are) and make it accessible to us ordinary men who have little time and sometimes less inclination to pursue such idealisms.

Most of what men know we have learned and male conditioning comes through the five senses. Men have been encouraged through what they hear, see, taste, feel and smell to become what society has required of them. The good and the bad have all been imprinted into the souls of men through the senses. If we are to make substantial changes in our lives we must begin by changing what we let into our selves. Care of the soul means taking responsibility to avoid what is toxic for our development and choosing to create opportunity and experiences that nourish us and encourage us towards a more wholesome and healthy masculinity.

What we see

How much beauty do most men see in the average day? Very little, I suspect. Men are taught not to dwell on such things. On the days that I drive my children to school I observe some interesting evidence of this. The road to the school is along a seafront that exhibits some of the most beautiful sunrises reflecting off the Clare hills and back into the water. Driving back to my house I am running against the rush-hour traffic all heading into the city to work. Most cars are occupied by men on their own, some by women and some by women bringing children to school. There is a very interesting ad hoc study here. Driving into beautiful scenic mornings, some misty wet, others bright and shimmering against the water, I watch the expressions. Most of the men look as if they are bracing themselves for some kind of adversity, the women look more interested in the surroundings, and those bringing children seem most relaxed and animated.

Most of the men just don't see the beauty. The reader will recall Terry, the man who had to relearn the difference between a job and a life discussed in an earlier chapter. The changes brought about through this crisis meant that he learned the importance of seeing. When he returned to work, he delighted in being able to stop his car on the way to meet a prospective client and take five minutes to sit and breathe in the fresh air, and look at the cloud formations over one of the most beautiful scenic areas in the country. He had learned to see. And he did better business.

Learning to see means choosing to give time to looking at things that are good for the soul. This includes what we read and watch on television and film. I am very partial to a good thriller but also realise that many films are actually designed to create a high level of emotional arousal including tension, fear and excitement. Others are enjoyed for their violence because they allow the watcher to feel the aggression of the protagonist without acting it out. Too much of this kind of a diet is bad for the soul and needs to be balanced by viewing quieter and more reflective material. My friend Norman has for years teased me about this issue. He tells me he'll know that I am cured of my predilection for the dark side when I start watching films like *Brigadoon*.

One of the seeing exercises that I encourage some clients to partake in takes two minutes a day (for many men anything longer is too much to begin with). It's very simple and yet many men immediately find themselves reacting to it. It involves going to a quiet room, or a chapel perhaps, lighting a candle, and watching the flame for two minutes while focusing on the flickering of the light as a symbol of the life within. The ever-changing light, its warmth, its shape and its power are all useful pictures of the light of life in our souls.

Tony had completed a few months of counselling with me. He

was a successful businessman, well thought of and respected by his peers and friends. His personal life was a shambles and he was in the midst of a very acrimonious separation. Attempting, as many do, to come up smelling of roses after the end of the relationship, he was leaving himself very vulnerable to a financial disaster in the separation settlement. Having worked on many of the pressing practical details, he was ready for some reflective therapy that would deepen his insight into himself and open up some possibilities for a deeper level of change. I recommended that he begin by doing this simple candle exercise for a few days in the time before the next session. He arrived back in good form, feeling that his life was beginning to shape up a bit better. He thanked me for my suggestion and told me that he had gone out and purchased the candles the day after the session.

I was somewhat surprised at the immediacy of the success. He went on to explain the reason for his gratitude. He didn't use them as planned but was grateful to have them on hand. There had been a power cut the week before and he had the means to illuminate his house! Typical male thinking, I thought. Candles are for light. All the other symbolic uses are a bit naff, a bit too spiritual for men like Tony.

Changing what we see means making choices that sometimes go against the grain. It means visiting an art gallery on occasion rather than the pub, it means watching a nature programme instead of the fifteenth news bulletin that day, it means reading something wholesome, a love story, a poem, a comedy, rather than another novel describing some serial killer on the loose brutalising and torturing his hapless victims. It means stopping the car and enjoying the sunset instead of rushing home stressed and uptight. It means a walk in the woods where the shape and colour of the leaves replace the inner angst of a new project. It means watching the faces of children instead of wishing they weren't in the way. And it all takes practice. Small changes can have very significant results.

What we hear

In a lot of cases we have little choice over what we hear, but a lot of freedom over what we listen to. Right now I can hear the tap tap of the keys on the word processor, in the distance there is a noise of traffic, and somewhere in the midst I can hear birdsong. Other household sounds, doors opening, phone ringing intermittently, interrupt these background noises. All of these sounds are entering my central nervous system but are given little attention because I am listening to a different sound, a noiseless one — the sound of my inner voice as it speaks the words I am writing.

Now I sit back and listen differently. After a moment of relaxing and focusing my attention I can pick out the birdsong. There are two birds close by, one sings at a higher pitch and is responded to by the other, then in the distance I become aware of another type of birdsong, to my untrained ear it sounds like a bigger bird, a blackbird perhaps, it fades in and out and I realise that it is taken to me by the wind. I hadn't noticed the wind sound until I started focusing. The traffic too has variety. There is some close by and I can get a sense of the speed, and the type of vehicle, and there is a more generalised distant noise like a low-level hum.

Listening is a choice about how we use the sense of hearing. When we take more control of this sense we can begin to listen for what is good for the soul. Care of the soul means listening for sounds that nourish it. When we listen to our loved ones, are we listening in order to find fault? are we listening to hear criticism? or are we listening to understand something about their soul? Men in general are taught to listen for information. Listening in this way is a functional activity to help us to do things better. This is of course a very important part of our sense of hearing but is deeply deficient as a means of healthy living. The sense of hearing is also given to us so that we can be enriched and comforted in our lives. We need to use it for these purposes also.

Changing what we listen to means using our sense of hearing, not just for information gathering but to help us grow in understanding our loved ones and in the appreciation of beauty. It means listening to music that speaks to the soul rather than distracts us. It means listening to good news, rather than the dramatised sound bites of infotainment news channels. It means listening to wisdom, to seminars on love and forgiveness on the tape deck in the car instead of some shallow radio quiz that promises T-shirts and dance CDs. It means listening for what is good, for what people wish to say instead of finishing their sentences for them.

Touch

Perhaps one of the most primal and significant of our senses, and yet the one most likely to be ignored and misused. Touch according to Nitya Lacroix transcends language and personality. It speaks directly to the innermost core of the human heart, soothing away pain and dissolving tension from body and mind. Touch is a powerful means of releasing internal turmoil and of receiving pleasure, comfort and consolation. Affectionate touch releases endorphins and boosts the immune system. Research confirms, for example, that elderly people who have affectionate touch contact with pets are more resistant to disease than those who do not receive any regular form of touch.

Men in particular suffer from a lack of touch in their everyday lives. This important means of stress release and affirmation is almost completely lacking for some men. For others, touch is available only through sexual encounter, which is a grave constriction of its place in human encounter. When we look at the high primates we see the role of touch as a crucial part of bonding. Gorillas, chimps and all other apes spend much time grooming each other as part of their communication. Modern men in the West are almost completely paranoid about touching each other. On a visit to Egypt I had some conversations with an Egyptian tour guide about the different ways that their culture seemed to allow men to have far more physical contact. It is a common sight to see men holding hands, touching each other while they talk and kissing each other when they meet. Such physical contact here could only be seen as homosexual in nature, and most of the Egyptian men I met were at pains to tell me that they were not gay.

Care of the soul means becoming more open to touch. This may mean being more affectionate with our loved ones, learning to become comfortable with more affectionate embraces, reassuring pats on the back, tousling our adolescent children's hair and so on. It also means learning to have our bodies anointed through therapeutic massage. Holistic massage has a long history and is recognised as a very important aspect of healthy self-care. From its first mention in the ancient Sanskrit texts, through the writing of Hippocrates in the fifth century on to the sixteen volumes on the topic by the Roman physician Galen, into the fourteenth century where it is recommended by eminent French physician Guy de Chaulic, to reach its present-day form in the works of Per Henrik Ling in the eighteenth century, the role of therapeutic touch is an important theme in keeping healthy. And in a culture that has almost forbidden touch to adult men and confined it to sexual intimate encounter we need to address this lack in our lives.

The sense of touch can also be accessed through awareness of the sensations of the body while walking, swimming or bathing. Many men walk as if they are not in their bodies. This is a legacy of the withdrawal of affection in the early years of boyhood, and the conditioning of such boys to become hardened to physical competition.

The role of touch in sexual communion is the most intimate and profound level of touch. Some men have difficulty in fully connecting to the role of touch when they make love with their partner. A key area of growth for such men is to learn how to linger in an embrace. Particular comment is made about the period after making love. Some commentators make fun of the scenario where a woman asks her lover what he is thinking just after they have reached climax and are in the afterglow. The likelihood is that some men are thinking thoughts that are so far away from the relationship that their partner would be hurt if they were truthful. The noise in the gearbox of the car, the chances of Manchester United winning the treble or the file that is left at the office may be the kinds of things that fill a man's mind in this situation. There is an important aspect to male functioning at work here and it relates directly to vulnerability. The experience of orgasm in a loving sexual encounter involves the collapse of ego boundaries and most men are extremely vulnerable and opened up emotionally as a result. We have seen earlier that it is ingrained into the male psyche that he respond to such vulnerability by putting the barriers of protection back up. Most do this by thinking about things that distract them from the intensity of their feelings.

Men, in general, need to learn to savour the sensual delight, the closeness and warmth of affectionate encounter with their lover. It has the power to heal in a very deep way some of the scars of early male conditioning. Philip came to see me because his marriage was in serious trouble. His wife, Tricia, had some sessions for herself and recounted the trouble they were having. She felt rejected and upset that Philip seemed to have no interest in the sexual side of their relationship. As we talked Philip revealed his great difficulty with touch. Raised with little or no affection, a cold mother and a hard-working practical father, he had no history of knowing the beauty of touch. He described waking up beside his lovely wife. Within a few seconds of becoming conscious his mind began to race in expectation of the day's work. Philip, another victim of the corporate cult, took no time or interest in waking up to the gentle feeling of closeness with his wife. I gave him a simple exercise to do. On waking up I suggested that he bring his attention into the feelings in his body and that he put his hand on his wife's body and try to begin an awareness of connection. He had to practise this for many mornings before he began to find his feelings changing and the beginnings of an emotional contact through touch.

Philip's experience is extreme, but is reflective of the way that some men can suffer a profound loss of one of life's great sources of healing and joy — the human touch.

It seems appropriate to complete this section on touch with some lines from Bruce Springsteen:

In the end what you don't surrender
Well the world just strips away
Ain't no kindness in the face of strangers
Ain't gonna find no miracles here
Well you can wait on your blessings my darling
But I got a deal for you right here

I ain't looking for your prayers or pity
I ain't coming round searching for a crutch
I just want someone to talk to
And a little of the human touch
Just a little of that human touch

Tell me in a world without pity
Do you think I'm asking too much
I just want someone to hold on to
And a little of the human touch
Just a little of that human touch.

Most men need to develop a new relationship to touch. And the best advice I can give is to focus on three affirmations — practise, linger and savour.

Smell

World-renowned neuropath Jan de Vries tells us that the sense of smell is the most neglected of the five senses in the modern world. Our relatives in the animal kingdom use smell constantly as a key part of their adaptation to their environment. We no longer need to use smell in this way and thus it is relinquished. This has some deep implications for health and well-being.

Smell is centrally connected to breathing. Taking in the breath is symbolic of the life-force within us. In a world full of pollution, of stressed people who breathe badly and who no longer focus their awareness of how they breathe, we need to relearn some of the importance of our sense of smell.

According to de Vries, the nasal cavity is directly related to the sympathetic nervous system. That system regulates all the key functions that are involuntary, including blood circulation, digestion, hormonal secretions and breathing. The endocrine system, which is particularly important in stress and anxiety, is directly connected to the nasal cavity. There are thus many good reasons to learn more about how to use the sense of smell to help with healthy living.

Here the focus is on care of the soul. The sense of smell was known for millennia to be an aid to spiritual practice. The ancient Egyptians in particular introduced the role of aromatic fragrance in most of their worship.

> Since the advent of institutional religions, places of worship have been infused with fragrances, from odorous wood balms and various essences intended to call upon the favour of the gods with their subtle fragrances. Cypress and cedar wood were burned in the temples of Mesopotamia while the smell of incense and rancid butter hangs in Tibetan monasteries. In India the air in sacred places is thick with the scent of sandalwood from which the holy statues are carved and the lotus flower unfolds its fragrant petals at the Buddha's feet. Rose and musk essences are enshrined in the heart of mosques while aromatic peppery basil haunts Orthodox places of worship. (From *The Book of Perfume* by Elisabeth Barille and Catherine Laroze.)

Those old enough to remember benediction can recall the use of incense to help us connect to God in devotion. Every Christmas we are reminded that the kings from the East brought frankincense and myrrh as gifts to the newborn saviour.

All of this tells us that the sense of smell has been considered throughout history to be a central element in spiritual worship. Perhaps the role of fragrance was to make us aware of breathing, and thus connect us to the deepest most primordial aspect of the breath, the tradition that tells us that it is through the breath that the spiritual enters the body. The book of Genesis tells us that God breathed life into Adam. In our breathing we are reminded of our spiritual nature. But our breathing is almost always out of our awareness. Fragrance makes the breath conscious and reminds us of our spirituality.

A third aspect of the sense of smell is the impact that aroma has on our emotional state. It is so easy to see this connection. Watch the expression on someone's face when they come across something that smells revolting. The face captures the emotion created by the smell. How does this work? In simple terms the olfactory epithelium contains more than twenty million nerve endings. Once a smell stimulates these nerve endings messages are sent directly to the master instrument — the hypothalamus — which sends messages to other parts of the brain, especially those connected with feelings and memory. Smell can thus be used as a key element in dealing with emotional states.

The gift of aromatherapy, now becoming the most commonly accessed of the complementary therapies, has known this for centuries. Skilled aromatherapists recognise the power of fragrance to work directly on the emotional and physical states of the person.

Care of the soul means working with smell in the following ways. We must learn to breathe properly. Yoga is the most commonly available tool to help proper life-enhancing breathing. There are instructional aids available, many in cassette form, that can be used to develop a healthier way of breathing.

Fragrances can be used to help us become aware of our spirituality. From the smell of new-mown hay to the flowers in the field to a good aftershave, we can stimulate our sense, and receive simple pleasure through the use of smell.

Essential oils are useful when we wish to use the sense of smell to heal some aspect of our lives. There are those that stimulate when we are feeling low and those that ease us when we are stressed and fearful. It costs so little to place an oil burner in our place of work, to put some cotton wool with healing fragrance in the air vents of the car. These are simple ways to rediscover and benefit from the healing and sensuous help of smell.

Taste

The sense of taste is given to us for protection. That which is bitter is more likely to be dangerous, and most natural sugar is very healthy and rich in energy and nutrition. The tongue is an amazing organ that has the dual function of testing what we imbibe, and making it possible to speak. Taste is about helping us to choose what to eat. And because our physical well-being is directly connected to our spiritual health we need to learn to savour what is good.

Care of the soul means care of the body. It means not feeding it junk, eating on the hoof, building up toxic waste in our cellular structure creating the increased likelihood of early death from cancer or heart disease. There is plenty being said about these issues so I will not labour the point here except to remind the reader that there are very serious problems around men's health that relate directly to bad eating habits.

Two other aspects of taste are, however, related to care of the soul. Addiction is a serious problem for some men. Addiction to alcohol, to cigarettes and to certain foods are all mediated by the sense of taste. A taste can be learned and we have to learn to like the taste of some things that are bad for us. Some of the more toxic potions we put into our bodies are initially rejected.

Remember those first few cigarettes? They tasted terrible. Our sense of taste tried to protect us by sending powerful reactions to the brain that said get that thing out of your mouth. Care of the soul means relearning to taste what is good.

Another aspect is that of comfort-eating. Touch and taste are the earliest senses that have immediate connection to the need for survival in the infant. Touch is profoundly important in cultivating in the infant a sense of trust as well as emotional bonding. Taste relieves the pain of hunger and comforts the child. This deep experience from infancy never really leaves us.

Many years ago I was working in the field of training and was requested to organise a corporate evening for a company I consulted with. Like most things I do, I did the best I could and tried to make sure everything was going well and people's needs were well provided for. Part of this was to ensure that the catering was of top quality. I was later told that I did too good a job. The food was elegantly laid out, with a wide variety of luxuries. I remember watching the company men arriving and indulging themselves. What struck me was that there seemed to be something awry with the way people were eating. I myself have had little time for food, seeing it as simply a fuel to provide energy for the important things in life. I witnessed something radically different in these men. They seemed to relish the food in some way that was bigger than the need to eat. It took me many years to realise that a lot of these men were unhappy, and stressed, and in fact were comfort-eating. They were getting emotional needs met through eating.

I have had to learn since that time that food is not simply fuel but is a source of pleasure in itself. The sense of taste affirms us that nourishing the body well is a thing of joy. Comfort-eating is a distortion of that process. Care of the soul means addressing the issues that make us overuse food to quell our inner angst, and fill up those empty spaces that some people refer to as the hole in the soul.

Summary

This chapter has focused on using the five senses as passageways to become more spiritually tuned and aware. Many of the suggestions are simple and practical but this belies their importance in healing some of the wounds that are intrinsic to manhood. By becoming more sensuous, pleasured, connected to the feelings in our bodies, we reduce the automatic tendency to stay in the world of ideas and thoughts. Important though these are they are overdeveloped in most men and are part of the imbalances that cause men many difficulties.

12 Purpose in Life

Introduction

In this chapter I will examine one of the key elements of human happiness, a sense of meaning in life. Many modern men have been handed a packaged meaning that belongs to a culture that needs them to operate from its tenets. Modern society tells men that their meaning is to accumulate, to be successful in its terms, and to provide quality of life for those who depend on them. On close examination, these meanings are insufficient and spiritually impoverished, because there is no place for that unique constellation that makes up any one person. These meanings are utilitarian, they are about being used for someone else's benefit. Warren Spielberg nicely summarises the dilemmas facing men around the issue of meaning. In 'Why men must be heroic' he writes:

> Perhaps the greatest difficulty many men face today involves the inability to construct for themselves an identity suffused with an authentic and integrated sense of life meaning . . . As traditional notions of masculinity fade in relevance, and as men have become more honest about their own personal histories and struggles, many have begun to question the meaning which they previously ascribed to their life . . . Unfortunately, however, most men have not been able to respond to the dilemma of a loss of a guiding image of manhood.

Men therefore are struggling to find a new basis for a worthwhile sense of meaning in life.

My interest in this area began almost twenty years ago. I could see even then that so much of modern psychology seemed to deny the possibility of a personal meaning for one's life. Most major schools of psychology saw people as products of their genetic inheritance and the luck of the draw as far as early environment was concerned.

The possibilities to transcend these conditions were seen as limited indeed. And yet such theories seem contradicted by much of what we know about the lives of people. More specifically, the example of great lives can teach us much about the meaning of one's own life. I don't mean here some religious or philosophical framework that suggests that there is one true meaning for human life in general. Such frameworks are well known. Islamic and Judaeo-Christian dogmas tell us that human meaning is largely about getting to know and love the creator God. Naturalism tells us that our primary purpose is to procreate the species or to simply find the best way to hand down one's genetic blueprint. Existentialism tells us that our meaning lies in courageously coping with meaninglessness — we are thrown into a chaotic and directionless universe and the absurd element in human nature is that we have faculties that make such meaninglessness intolerable. Our purpose is to be heroic and authentic in the face of this absurdity. Other 'isms' tell us that we are in a process of continual improvement and we go through many existences on the way to eternal bliss.

These are some of the more popular belief systems that have developed over the history of human thought as ways to help people to come to terms with the problem of meaning. Each offers a system of meaning that is universal, in other words each makes claims about the meaning of people's lives, each has its merits and each has its dark side. In this chapter I am not discussing these larger philosophical and religious movements and dogmas. Rather, I am examining the issue of meaning in terms of a specific meaning for one's own personal existence. If we strive to take away the cultural conditioning that for centuries has shaped the lives of men and told them their purpose, we must replace this with a meaning that has more to offer. For every man this direction will have its own unique character.

The importance of meaning

I have long been sceptical of the notion that my life has some purpose that was carved out for me in some form that pre-existed my birth. There seems to be far too much suffering, chaos and depravity in the world to suggest that people in general and myself in particular are working according to some Divine or Demonic plan. A more recent development that has rekindled my scepticism is the popular notion that my life is an incarnation, or embodiment, of a soul that has chosen its parents, and its time of arrival. These ideas, which were once the province of myth and magic, are now coming into the mainstream of what is loosely termed New Age thinking. Alongside this resistance, and travelling parallel to it, is the deep sense that my existence on this planet cannot simply be reduced to some genetic accident that happened to give me the personality that I now have. I think we can come to some resolution of these opposing forces by saying that a person's life can have a meaning and purpose that exists by virtue of his or her existence. We do not have to resort to other worlds to explain such purpose (although you can if you wish).

A personal meaning for one's life is an extraordinary gift. It gives direction to one's choices, it provides a deep sense of satisfaction and it cultivates a healthy form of independence and individuality. It promotes emotional and spiritual health and it is a source of comfort and consolation as death approaches. Most people need to know that their lives have meaning, yet few are prepared to undertake an original quest. Sometimes this is because they are too lazy and prefer to accept the pre-packaged versions handed down through religious tradition or a particular school of philosophical thought. Sometimes it is because they fear that such a quest could lead to despair and sometimes it is because they just don't know how to approach the problem. It is these last people to whom this chapter is addressed. While much of the content here concerns people in general there is a bias towards those areas that are of particular relevance to men. Briefly then this chapter is about how to find a personal purpose for one's life. In my work on this topic over the years several themes have emerged. These are: developing a sense of uniqueness, taking responsibility and tolerating suffering. Each of these has a key part to play in knowing and in following one's purpose in life.

Developing a sense of uniqueness

Purpose in life is locked into the unique nature of the individual. I like James Hillman's work on this topic although disagreeing with some aspects, particularly those concerning the role of angels. His acorn theory is, however, a wonderfully poetic way of describing the uniqueness of each human being. After a rather scathing attack on modern psychology Hillman states:

> This book refuses to leave to the lab of psychology that sense of individuality at the core of 'Me'. Nor will it accept that my strange and precious human life is the result of statistical chance . . . The acorn theory proposes that you and I and every single person is born with a defining image. Individuality resides in a formal cause — to use old philosophical language going back to Aristotle. We each embody our own idea, in the language of Plato and Plotinus. And this form, this idea, this innate image does not tolerate too much straying.

Hillman's acorn theory is, despite his anger with a lot of psychology, very similar to the self theory of Rogers and Maslow that began that extraordinary development called the Third Force in psychology in the late sixties. The common ground lies in the notion that despite all the effects of environment there is within each human being a unique self that wants to grow and find expression in the world. Philosopher Karl Jaspers is succinct in his explanation that 'at some decisive point every individual is as it were, in theological language, created from a source of his own and not merely the processing of a modified hereditary substance'.

I am inclined to agree with this way of looking at people. I believe, however, that it is possible for a person to live out the whole of their lives and not express that self. Instead they can construct a functional self to respond to the demands, expectations and coaxing of their environment. That constructed self can become their prison, locking much that is unique about them into a cellar in the unconscious, left to wither and die, depriving the person, and the world, of the gifts that were inherent in his or her existence. To bring Hillman's theory together with the parable of the sower, the acorn can land on stony soil that eventually defeats its potential for becoming a beautiful oak. A person's true self can lie dormant beneath fear, laziness or simple ignorance. People can spend their lives dancing to the beat of someone else's music. They will, in general, become sick and probably die young. Bernie Siegal summarises this all too common tragedy very well when he says, 'If, when you are on your deathbed, someone else's life flashes before your eyes then you know you got it wrong.'

So, what kind of oak tree does your acorn want to grow into? Two directions can help you to get the picture: one involves looking back and the other involves looking forward. Looking back at childhood is an important step in getting to know the nature of the true self. Before the mighty hand of social forces and the inevitable shaping through education, authority, structured learning, with all the potential for suppression, misdirection and mediocrity, took its toll, there was a child who imagined its place in the world through fantasy, who daydreamed at night, who drew absent-minded figures and scenes on the back of his copybook. In all that imagining and imaging lies a pattern that tells you of your self. Take time to remember the child. He has much to tell you of your self.

Looking forward means projecting into the future so that you can look back. One exercise that is very effective in finding some important themes that lie in your acorn is to write your obituary. I was at the funeral of my close friend Owen's mother recently. His brother Tony gave a moving and beautiful summary of this woman's life. He spoke of her unselfishness, her capacity for love and her spirituality. Her last years were spent in a nursing home and in his final conversation with her, he asked her if she was lonely. Her answer was a deep tribute to her meaning in life. She replied, 'No, I pray for ye all the time.' Tony understood this to mean that his mother kept herself in their company through her prayers. In his eulogy he talked about how well her reply seemed to summarise much of what he knew his mother to be, a woman of great compassion, of deep loyalty, who did not waver or become bitter even though her life involved much pain and suffering.

What do you want to have said about you when you are being laid to rest? Do you want to be remembered for the hundreds of hours spent improving your golf stroke, for the killing you made on the stock exchange, for being the best snooker player, or do you wish to be remembered for something else? Writing your obituary has the effect of helping you to see what you really want to live for, even if on a day-to-day basis you are not putting any energy into it.

A third task is one that I am taking from Sam Keen's book *Fire in the Belly*. This involves writing a hall of fame, making a list of the people you most admire.

> Our personal halls of fame are made up of our private heroes, saints and models. Think of your hall of fame as a

> house of mirrors, each of which gives you a glimpse of some aspect of yourself. It may contain people whose names are in the news, men and women you admire because they are beautiful, powerful, talented, smart, wise or compassionate. But it will also contain a more intimate group of friends, parents, teachers and lovers who have enriched your lives with their special gifts of care, insight and understanding . . . Each person's hall of fame is made up of a unique cast of characters because it reflects the self's ideal. Tell me who you admire and I will tell you what kind of a person you aspire to become.

When making this list it is important to realise that some may feature in it because they possess a quality you admire, even if there are other aspects of the character that you dislike or disrespect. Be inclusive rather than exclusive, and then try to summarise the picture that is emerging. As you do your daily round try to remember this picture. You may be surprised at the impact it will have on your life. As Hillman wisely comments, 'Often the demands of the calling ruthlessly wreak havoc on the decencies of a well-lived life.'

Taking responsibility

Taking responsibility here refers to the task of responding to the purpose that begins to emerge as you learn more about the call. How do we respond to the growing urgency that tells us that our lives must change direction if we are to fulfil our meaning? How can we be responsible if the call involves moving house, changing jobs, taking risks, ending relationships? Surely responsibility is about being consistent, keeping commitments, not doing anything that would jeopardise the lives of those who depend on us? In general, this is what we hear when we hear the words take responsibility.

There are a few things worth saying about this. Firstly, the world we live in is a construction. Many of the concepts that are held so dear are sacred cows constructed at the foot of the mountain because we in the West could not wait for wiser solutions to the changes that occurred as a result of the Industrial Revolution. The nuclear family, life insurance, nine to five, thirty-five-hour work week, mortgages, sun holidays, traffic chaos, unemployment, pollution and so on — all key elements that determine most of our ways of being in the world — are a construction of industrial and technological societies. When we look at the issue of responsibility we must look at what we are being responsible to. In a different world we might be responsible to share our crops, to learn the ways of the shaman, to gather together and feast the harvest, to take boys from their mothers and teach them the ways of the warrior. In simple terms then, the commonly accepted social rules are not written in stone.

To lose your purpose because of a fear of not conforming to a social construction is a great mistake. John O'Donohoe in that eloquent book on Celtic spirituality *Anam Cara* says that

> one of the greatest sins is the unlived life. We are sent into the world to live to the full everything that comes towards us. It is a lonely experience to be at the deathbed of someone who is full of regret; to hear him say how he would have loved another year to do the things his heart had always dreamed of but believed he could never do until he retired. There are many people who do not live the lives they desire. Many of the things that hold them back from inhabiting their destiny are false. These are only images in their minds. They are not real barriers at all. We should never allow our fears and the expectations of others to set the frontiers of our destiny.

Secondly, things take time. If your calling requires significant change in life circumstances such as a new career, leaving a marriage, getting married, having children, travelling or any other major shifts of direction, then being responsible means planning, it means being patient, it means recognising the impact that these changes may have on the lives of others. It means minimising the pain caused to others who may have invested their lives in your maintaining the status quo, while still staying the course of change.

Thirdly, much of the change that can occur as part of the calling may be internal. It may have less to do with shifting one's life circumstances and more to do with developing character. Part of this may require becoming free of aspects that trip you up spiritually and psychologically. This sometimes means facing very difficult internal demons, some of which may have lain dormant in the psyche since childhood. Taking responsibility means facing up to the inner struggles, the depressions, the anxieties, and sometimes the wounds inflicted through abuse or neglect. It may mean facing up to one's addictions. Addiction by its very nature is a form of enslavement. It is the replacement of meaning and can use you up till you wither and die. Some people seem to manage these difficulties on their own, for others taking responsibility can mean getting help with these struggles. Much of what is written in another book of mine, *Healing Life's Hurts*, can be of value here.

There is an important warning that I passionately believe needs to be made with regard to healing and therapeutic work. Doing therapy is not a calling. Therapy is supposed to be a time of healing, a lancing of the abscess of all the trapped emotional toxins of childhood, and a chance to learn how to live more freely. It is a means to an end. Therapy does not provide meaning. Its function is to clear the path so that one can pursue one's calling uninhibited by the psychic pitfalls and traps of developmental dysfunction. The great mistake of modern psychotherapy, and of many psychotherapists and counsellors, is that they conclude that the process of releasing, analysis, visualisation and so on will make a person well. This is not necessarily true, being well means knowing how to live an authentic life, and part of that is the spiritual maturing and vocation that I have described in these chapters.

Psychotherapy does not provide a calling, it may clarify it but the process of working on oneself in therapy is not sufficient as a basis for one's meaning in life. Not to see this important limitation often results in therapy becoming an end in itself. People become devotees of their own therapy which leads them further and further into narcissistic self-indulgence. Going from workshop to workshop, from therapist and healer to another therapist and healer, the person loses sight of the reason for being in therapy in the first place. Some therapists are qualified to move on from their role in helping people heal the wounds from their past into the role of becoming their spiritual directors and helping them to know how to live authentically in the present. Many are not. The tasks are very different and it is important to recognise this if you engage in getting help.

A place for suffering

Making a place for suffering is part of the calling because it is inherent in the human condition. Much suffering is unnecessary and leads to sickness and despair. And yet, for men making the transitions being discussed here, there are some aspects of suffering that must be integrated into their development. Failure to face authentic suffering is often the basis for addiction, acting out, violence and many other forms by which people's lives can be destroyed. Mortality is the obvious example. For many men the gradual deterioration of their physical energy, strength and power is deeply traumatic. Having defined themselves by their performance, achievement and drive they now face the inevitable loss of all these defining qualities. In the modern world the cult of youthism discards the elderly. There is no dignity any longer in being an old man. All the wisdom that has accumulated, wisdom that would tell young men not to follow the illusions that are given to men, wisdom that might explain how ultimately banal and empty are so many of the promises inherent in how to be a man, wisdom that would help young men grow, as Jesus did from the age of seven, 'in wisdom and in stature', all this wisdom is lost, thrown away as the ramblings of some old fool.

Others never get wise, it's too painful and it's too late to allow oneself to see the waste of oneself. So the trappings of success allow for a comfortable nursing home, an adequate supply of medication, and hopefully more visits from the family. The great opportunity that lies in knowing and pursuing one's meaning in life is that it leaves us able to integrate the reality of our deaths into our lives. As most of the existentialists tell us, one cannot know how to live if we do not know how to die.

A certain form of loneliness is a necessary form of suffering. For some men this is deeply traumatic and avoided at all costs. The loneliness I am referring to can best be described using that great expression 'the dark night of the soul'. There is a time that a man must be prepared to live through when he feels utterly alone and abandoned. This is the time that he takes when he moves inward and does battle with himself, with his own frailty and vulnerability, when he comes to meet the shadow, his dark destructive side. The pain of this loneliness is always about being alone with oneself. It is the time of grief when he recognises that he has been sold out, that his life energies have been mortgaged and that now he must reclaim them. If he lets himself get through this time without allowing people to medicate him or tell him some silly story about mid-life crises he will emerge as the owner of his own life.

Coming to terms with limitations is a form of suffering similar to that of dealing with one's mortality. All freedom is a freedom within limitations. One of these limitations is the experience of loss. Every choice we make has a loss of other choices built into its fabric. As I have said elsewhere, loss is an inevitable part of the process of living. The only relationship we will never lose is our relationship with ourselves. Everything else goes. Children grow up and move away, spouses leave or die, parents die, friends sometimes due to life circumstances are no longer available and as the years go on it is harder to make new ones. Jobs change, downsizing makes redundancies, and so on. Learning to look bravely into the face of loss and not shirk its painful thrusts is important. Denial always comes back to bite you on the bum. Alcohol and other drugs when used to facilitate denial eventually diminish the soul. There is no yellow brick road that takes away the reality of loss and leads us into some other world of happiness. The world of fantasy is dangerous to men who live the present dreaming about the future. Caring for the soul means being able to grieve loss well, to let go rather than frantically try to hold on, and to accept its part as a price of being alive. Then it loses some of its sting.

If there are times in all of this focus on life's purpose when there is a sense of regret and loss then grief is important but it is equally important to arise from it and move on. In Charles Frazier's beautiful novel about endurance and love *Cold Mountain* the central character Inman describes this well.

> He told her about the first time he had looked at the back of her neck as she sat in the church pew. Of the feeling that had never let go of him since. He talked to her of the great waste of years between then and now. A long time gone. And it was pointless to think of how those years could have been put to better use for he could hardly have put them to worse. There was no recovering them now. You could grieve endlessly for the loss of time and the damage done therein. For the dead and for your own lost self. But what the wisdom of the ages says is that we do well not to grieve on and on. And those old ones knew a thing or two and had some truth to tell, Inman said, for you could grieve your heart out and in the end you are still where you were. All your grief hasn't changed a thing. What you have lost will not be returned to you. It will always be lost. You're left with only your scars. All you can

do is choose to go on or not. But if you go on, it's knowing you are carrying your scars with you.

Summary

This chapter has examined the major changes that are required in the internal working of men if they are to be released from the conditioning of the past, and still retain their dignity and wisdom as men. Men who know how to care for their soul and invest their time and energy in doing so will become the kind of men that will make the world a better and gentler place to live in, for themselves, and for those who live with them. They will also have the resources to engage in the beautiful and enriching experiences that are described in the remainder of this book.

13 Deepening Friendship

Introduction

Perhaps one of the most life-enhancing and treasured experiences that human beings can have is a significant and long-lasting friendship. I am deeply grateful to have friends that I cherish, who have hung in there with me through the years of enormous change, struggle and growth. Friends that all played important roles in my development and healing over the past fifteen to twenty years. We have discussed earlier the intensity of bonding that can occur in men's lives when they are pitted together against adversity. Songs from Rolf Harris's 'Two Little Boys' to Dire Straits' 'Brothers in Arms', literature from Primo Levi's *If This is a Man* to Sebastian Faulks's *Birdsong* attest to the beauty of male friendship. This chapter looks at some ways that men can improve and deepen their friendships, rather than letting them stagnate and wither from lack of nurturing care.

Male friendship

A great number of men are lonely. Part of the reason for this is that most men do not know how to make the best of their friendships. Others have no true friends. It is a profoundly felt loss to the men I talk with that at the age of forty or fifty they have no other man in their lives that they can share their hurts, worries and achievements with. So many men keep all this within, even if they do have a comrade who is a true friend. Why is this such a common and destructive experience? Sam Keen is deeply insightful when he says:

> Within the community of men, I have learned that men's loneliness is a measurement of the degree to which we have ignored the fundamental truth of interdependence. In devoting ourselves to getting, spending, and being entertained, we simply forget that we inevitably feel alienated when we do not live within a circle of friends, within the arms of a family, within the conversation of a community. There is no way we can recover a secure sense of manhood without rediscovering the bonds that unite us to others and reaffirming our fidelity to the 'We' that is an essential part of the 'I'. To pretend that a man standing tall and alone is virile is to base our view of manhood on a metaphysic of separation that has been shown to be an illusion by almost every advance of the physical and social science of our era.

Part of the way out of loneliness is for men to understand that friendship is a special form of living relationship, and that like all living things it needs to be nurtured, fed and cared for. In so many experiences of life this reality is left unspoken. A lovely summary is found in *The Little Book of Calm*: 'Remind yourself that the most common deathbed regrets relate to neglected relationships not unfinished business.'

The world of film, for example, is marked out by a consistent theme of adolescent men from Mel Gibson to Bruce Willis, Steven Seagal to Wesley Snipes acting like invulnerable paper cut-out heroes. What is lacking in depth, in plot and in meaning is made up for with better special effects and dramatic pyrotechnics. The characters these men play don't operate in the realm of developed masculinity or true friendship and one eventually despairs of finding some indication that this popular medium which has a wide male audience can speak on this subject. And then along comes a jewel of a film that gives us a useful and eloquent message about male friendship. *The Shawshank Redemption* is one such film. The central character,

Andy Dufresne, ends up with a life sentence in Shawshank prison. The story revolves around his patient refusal to be broken by the prison system. The film has a particular resonance for me. A friend, who knows my soul, told me after he had seen it that this characterisation reminded him of me. Andy Dufresne is a bookish, intense and gentle soul, and with his little rock hammer chips away at his prison wall until he finds his freedom. This is not an inaccurate metaphor for much of my life experience. That aside, what can we learn about friendship from this film?

The Shawshank Redemption is one of the great stories about men. It has it all. The brutality and the violence is reflected by 'the sisters', a gang of three or four prisoners whose predilection is to choose a particular prisoner from the crop of new arrivals, who is then raped with regularity. And the advice is to accept this as one's lot or risk savage beating. Andy is one of their victims. Savagery is reflected in the prison guards, tough, unkind men cauterised by years of violation with no care or respect for the prisoners. Calculated cruelty and greed is depicted by the prison warden, a regular stand-up guy. You could be praying next to him at church and not see the devil in his heart.

Endurance is characterised by 'Red', who goes to his parole hearings, every few years, is polite and knows that there is no salvation, and freedom will not be granted. A beautifully scripted passage shows him keep his dignity after forty years in prison. The passage is worth quoting as it has something to say about nobility, about maintaining integrity in the face of suffering, and it has something to say about young men needing wise men to help them avoid mistakes that can cost them dearly.

The parole board hearing gets under way with three relatively young parole board officials.

Parole Officer: Boyd Reading, you have served forty years of a life sentence. Do you feel you have been rehabilitated?

Red:	Rehabilitated: Well let me see. You know I don't have any idea what that means.
Parole Officer:	Well it means you are ready to rejoin society and . . .
Red:	I know what you think it means, sonny. To me it's just a made-up word, a politician's word, so that young fellas like yourself can wear a suit and tie, have a job. What do you really want to know? Am I sorry for what I did?
Parole Officer:	Well are you?
Red:	There's not a day goes by that I don't feel regret, not because I'm in here or because you think that I should; I look back on the way I was then, a young stupid kid, who committed that terrible crime, I want to talk to him, I want to try to talk some sense into him, tell him the way things are, but I can't. That kid is long gone, and this old man is all that's left, I gotta live with that. Rehabilitation is just a bullshit word — so you go on and stamp your forms, sonny, and stop wasting my time because to tell you the truth I don't give a shit.

Kindness and compassion is reflected in Brooks, the prisoner who sets free his pet crow that has been his companion for years after he found him as a young hatchling. Brooks is so institutionalised that he cannot leave and kills himself on his release into a world that has completely changed. Enthusiasm and passionate idealism is given to the young hopeful, who on entering the prison is encouraged to do his high school diploma only to be murdered for threatening the system. Vision and perseverance mark out Andy as he seeks to have a library created within the prison. And amid all this loss, sorrow, anguish, a diamond gleams in the murk as we see a love grow between Andy Dufresne and Red. Red waits patiently and worries for his friend in solitary confinement, he grows to trust in his innocence, they talk of deep things, and they keep each other's hopes alive. Few films deserve the happy ever after ending, but this one does.

We can take several useful themes about male friendship from this film. Friendship takes time, friendship is based on respect, friendship involves communication and friendship means co-operation. Let us look at each briefly.

Friendship takes time

When did you last plan to spend a significant amount of time with a friend simply to enjoy his company? Men are notoriously bad at giving friendship this kind of priority. A good friendship takes years to evolve into a deep and abiding connection, and each of those years needs to contain time just for being with each other. I remember several years ago planning to take some time away with my friend Bruno. We spent a week together in Portugal, and made our then good friendship into a lifetime bond. Our greatest challenge was to convince the locals that we weren't gay. Close male friendship is so rarely presented to the world that when it is there is an automatic assumption that such men are homosexuals.

All the time in the world will not, however, make a friendship work well if a person doesn't know how to communicate at this level. And one of the great barriers to male communication is competition.

Stop competing

One of the most toxic diseases that undermines male friendship, especially in its early stages, is that of competition. When men compete in their relationship each is jockeying for a position, each is trying to establish a level of superiority over the other. This can include resenting areas where the other is more developed, achievements he has mastered, or even down to such basic things as the fact that he has more money or a bigger car. The underside of this competitive streak is that of shame. Competition prevents honest communication because it infects the relationship with a fear of exposure. The subtle judgments that then take hold gradually create a toxic atmosphere that is usually disguised beneath what men call slagging. Put-downs, subtle criticisms, pent-up jealousy, fear of exposure all take more and more hold as the relationship gradually disappears. It is rare for such relationships to end with an honest discussion, rather the men in them tighten their armour and withdraw.

Listen and talk

Two of the great skills of relationship building, listening and talking, are essential parts of nurturing friendship. And yet many men don't use them. Take a trip down to your local pub and watch men relate. I can do this research in my own special haunt, Mick Byrne's pub. This is a pub that generates a friendly and congenial atmosphere, mainly as a result of Mick's own larger-than-life personality and his warmth. There you will meet men who know each other for decades. Some have deep respect and care for each other. When they talk they talk trivia. When one of them dies he is mourned and profoundly missed. And throughout the hundreds of hours of time spent together many will not have revealed themselves in any substantial way. Many will have kept their worries, their hopes and their dreams to themselves, letting none of these people really know them. This is the legacy of male conditioning.

Most men do not know how to talk intimately with each other. Better friendship means learning this art. I am not here suggesting that we turn male friendships into some kind of Americanised encounter group. There is a balance somewhere between the tight-lipped fear-based need to keep one's heart concerns to oneself at all cost, and some of the grotesque examples of spilling one's guts we see on that banal and deeply troubling phenomenon — confessional television.

Learning the art of more intimate communication means taking risks. It means speaking from the heart rather than from the head. It means selecting someone you trust and when you feel the resistance that tells you to hide, making that courageous leap and opening up. It means learning to ask questions and listening to the answers, and it means being prepared to tell the other how you feel about him. These are such basic things but they are the keys to enriching and advancing the relationship. Choosing to talk about the content of this book for example might make for a good beginning.

Affirming and confronting each other

Friendship contains responsibility to each other's lives. There is an important distinction between being responsible for someone and responsible to someone. The former when it concerns adult relationships leads to codependency because once we take responsibility for another adult we have lost our independence and have begun to try to control them. This is a dysfunction. Being responsible to another is, however, an essential part of valuing them as a friend. Such responsibility means doing things that help. These may be practical things, which for most men are the easiest option. Lending a hand at some project or other, analysing together some plan or other conundrum. More difficult affirmations are those that involve encouragement, praise, gift giving and gestures of appreciation. Feeling at ease while telling a male friend that you love them, that you value them highly and that they are really important in your life is as yet a faraway possibility for many men.

True friendship sometimes means being courageous enough to tell a friend something they do not want to hear — some issue that offends you, some way in which they are being blind and taking risks that may damage themselves or others or the friendship itself. Such confrontations need to be rare happenings but are a part of the responsibility of friendship.

Learning about mythical friendships

One way to keep the issue of male friendship fresh in one's mind is to read up on the close male friendships that are spoken of in many mythical traditions. In these writings we get to see just how important male friendship is in the consciousness of human history and how it seems that in the modern world we are particularly impoverished in this area. David and Jonathan are soulmates in the Old Testament. The Holy Writ tells us that 'the soul of Jonathan was knit to the soul of David and Jonathan loved him as himself' (1 Samuel 18:1); Jesus tells us in John 15:13 that 'Greater love hath no man than this, that a man lay down his life for his friends.' Our own Celtic mythology contains one of the most dramatic and beautiful stories of male friendship, that of Ferdia and Cuchulainn.

William Doty in an article called 'Companionship thick as trees: our myths of friendship' provides a fitting closure to this chapter. He instructs us as to the learning that can occur when we look at the historical and mythological accounts of male friendship.

> To be sure, historical and mythological instances of friendship denote only some of the highway markers guiding where we may go. When our hearts open out to others beyond the couple bond, such openness begins to appear not as threatening but as enriching possibilities of being 'more human' than we can be within narrowly specified relationships. Something . . . then begins to be conceivably anew: demanding that we might be courteous, humane, affable and gentle in our associations with others. Reminding us that we must be active and diligent in serving and caring for the welfare and honour of our friends. Tolerating their defects yet joining them in the birthing of

relational significances that just may enable us to recover anew those sacred bonds of friendship that will reawaken our perception of the handsome inner qualities of one another. And revitalizing the ancient joys of having friends till death do us part.

Summary

This chapter has examined briefly the phenomenon of male friendship. It suggests that men in general need to learn to nurture and develop their friendships. The conditioning of men has led to a failure to learn the art of intimacy in the context of male friendship, a fear of exposure, and a tendency to leave friendships without the care and attention that could best help them to flourish. In consequence, much of the beauty, healing and powerful encouragement that can inhere in a close bond of friendship with a soul brother is something many men live out their lives without. This does not have to be the case.

14 Intimacy and Sexuality

Introduction

It seems appropriate that this chapter follows on friendship. An important aspect of the kind of intimate relationships that men build with their lovers is that it not be the complete source of companionship. This can put too much pressure on the relationship. Men who have close male friends are in a better place to cultivate and sustain a deep and enriching sexual partnership. This chapter examines some of the central elements in building such relationships and particularly focuses on the blocks that many men have within. These are there as a result of their formative influences and become obstacles to intimacy. Before discussing these difficulties I must first address the issue of homosexuality.

Homosexuality

No discussion of male sexuality and intimacy can be validly undertaken without recognising that homosexuality is a form of intimate sexual relationship that is distinct from opposite-sex relationship. Most of what is said in this book thus far is directly relevant to all men whether homosexual or heterosexual. The content of this chapter is, however, focused primarily on heterosexual relationships between men and women. This is so for two reasons. Firstly, at a simply practical level, the majority of men are heterosexual. Secondly, I don't have a lot to say about the nature of gay love and intimacy. This is because I don't know much about it. Yes, I have read the literature. The arguments from genetics tell us that homosexuality is genetic in origin. Research on rats shows that if testosterone is manipulated *in utero* at the time that the genetic messengers for sex typing are taking effect then the adult rats that emerge will mount other male rats. The old Freudian theory about strong mothers driving boys into the arms of men is another view, which is generally unsupported. I don't think the mounting behaviour of rats or the musings of a rather brilliant but biased Austrian doctor at the turn of this century can enlighten us much on such a complex subject.

One thing is certain, however, all men have some reaction to homosexuality. My own is a mixture of curiosity, respect, confusion and a recognition that I will never understand it. I heard a prominent intellectual who is in the public eye and is also homosexual in a debate recently with some fundamentalist and conservative clergymen. He devastated their arguments and one of his telling points was the discussion of what it is that causes people to react so strongly to male homosexuality. He said that everyone seems to agree that close male friendship, affection and even love is a good thing. It is the physical reality of sexual behaviour that causes people to react. I tend to agree with him.

The notion of one man lying in bed fondling the penis of another in a loving embrace is something that disgusts many people. The reality of anal sex between two men (even though many men enjoy anal sex with a woman) is even more traumatic an image for some. On reflecting on this I realised that I have a different reaction to lesbian love than I do to male homosexuality. I remember being in London a few years ago and getting on a tube train late at night. The train was delayed at the station and I watched (somewhat surreptitiously) two young women lovers kiss in a long lingering erotic sort of way. I thought it was beautiful and sensuous. If it had been two men I would have had some tolerance but very little sense of it as a beautiful and positive thing.

Just as it is impossible for a male to truly understand a female it is in my opinion impossible for a heterosexual male to fully understand the experience of homosexuality. I have close male friends, we can be expressive, affectionate and warm with each other. We can hug each other, say that we love each other and we can experience profound communion and fellowship. And yet I cannot imagine ever wishing to make that into a sexual exchange. This tells me something, that there is an experience within homosexuality that is beyond my understanding. There is a beautiful moment in the film *Midnight Express* that reflects this point. Amid the awful cruelty and degradation of a Turkish prison the men grow to love each other deeply. They are lonely and desperately in need of love and affection. In one scene the main character washes his friend. He moves the cloth tenderly and affectionately over his body. They are both naked and the other begins to respond very sensitively and sexually to this loving touch. He wants to kiss, and I have never seen a more appropriate moment portrayed in film for such a kiss to take place. And yet the other character, gently and somewhat sadly, refuses, saying, 'I am not like that.' It is not a judgment or a criticism, just a fact. In the remainder of this chapter I will discuss sex and intimacy with the important caveat that the sexual and intimate encounters between homosexual or bisexual men will need to be discussed elsewhere by someone who understands it better.

Men loving women

It is interesting that so many books talk of the failure that men encounter in their attempts to love women. The literature focuses less on the issue of women knowing how to effectively love men. It seems to be a popular opinion that men lack some fundamental quality when it comes to building and sustaining intimate sexual relationship. One myth has it that men are not interested in committed relationships. I think this is inaccurate. Another tells us that men are unable to express feelings towards women. Still another claims that men are interested only in sex and all the other paraphernalia of relationships are simply accepted as part of what is needed in order to keep the sex available. Comedian Billy Connolly humorously captures this conundrum when he says, 'Experts tell us that men get to intimacy through sex, whereas women get to sex through intimacy, so we're f*****d to begin with.' While there are elements of truth in all these generalisations none is of much help when a man seeks to understand how he can enhance the quality of his relationship with his lover.

There are important differences between men and women in their way of approaching relationships. But I believe that most men and most women are seeking the same goals: a consistent, enjoyable, loving sexual relationship that grows and deepens over the years. The easiest part of this discussion is the area of sexual expression. Most men want to be good lovers. Most men enjoy the pleasure they can give, and once again like all areas of male functioning there is an element of wanting to achieve success. Insecure men are more likely to be nervous about their sexual competence. This nervousness can range from whether or not they can make their lover climax (I'm aware of the feminist dictum 'We are responsible for our own orgasms') to worries about the size of their penis. Many such nervous men can encounter sexual difficulties, premature ejaculation in particular because there is a performance anxiety attached to their sexual encounters.

The enormous changes in attitudes to sex have liberated people in their sexual expression. There is no longer any need for sexual hang-ups to cripple relationships. Everywhere we look there is information available on the technical aspects of good sex. More and more books adorn the bookshelves telling us how to improve orgasm, how to pleasure each other and how to do 'it' in sixty-four different ways. Television programmes take us to the holiday spots and follow the antics of the young and beautiful. These programmes are the closest thing I can imagine to filming a human rutting season. There are no hang-ups, no worries, you can have sex on the beach while listening to songs about sex on the beach. A recent Sunday newspaper is instructive. In a week when a well-loved young TV celebrity was shot dead by a hit man, when nail bombs killed members of a wedding party at a gay pub, when a million Kosovan refugees continued suffering, when NATO intensified its war against Serbia, and a plethora of other significant world events took place, the headlines of the paper tell us that an eighteen-year-old member of a popular boy band had sex five times in one night with a raunchy barmaid. Pages 2 and 3 gave explicit accounts of what happened and how. It read like something that would have been considered pornographic not so long ago. In a small corner of the front page we read about the communal grave of sixty-two young boys brutalised and neglected in an orphanage run by a religious order in the west of Ireland until the 1960s.

There is something instructive in all this. Sex is no longer a matter of privacy and modesty, it is strewn around us in every way, shape and form. The positive element in this is that the shame and fear that so many men encountered as part of their sexuality is no longer prevalent. The negative element is that sex is becoming increasingly focused on performance and further separated from relationship. While all around us sex is being marketed, a great number of men are lonely and unfulfilled in their relationships. It is fine to know how to perform well sexually, it is of no real value when there is no one in your life that you can enjoy this encounter with. This brings us to the issue of intimacy.

At the end of the day most men know that playing around with sex for its own sake eventually becomes a hollow and empty experience. Most men want regular sex, but want it in the context of a loving relationship. It is in such a relationship that the security exists to learn to improve sexual communication, that the level of emotional and spiritual communion increases which in turn has a dramatic effect on the intensity, pleasure and euphoria of lovemaking. The keys to establishing such relationships are far more difficult than learning how to be a good lover. The latter is a matter of education and practice that can be accessed through books and videos that deal with the art of sexual performance. If there are significant sexual difficulties they can be discussed with a therapist qualified to help in these areas. Most sexual difficulty and dissatisfaction is, however, a result of a problem with intimacy. And it is here that men's conditioning can be a grave obstacle.

Building and sustaining intimacy

In general, male difficulties around intimacy involve difficulties with affection, communication, unrealistic expectations that often lead to conflict. Each of these areas is crucial to building and sustaining intimacy. Before discussing these it is important to note that many aspects of relationships have changed radically over the past few decades. There are many reasons why people choose each other for marriage or long-term relationship. And there are many reasons why some people stay together. Until recently, powerful forces ensured that people stayed together even if deeply unhappy. Two of these forces were economic and social pressure. Enormous numbers of unhappy relationships were played out till death did eventually give them blessed relief, which puts a slightly different meaning on the commitment 'till death do us part'.

Social pressure came in the form of religious beliefs. Most couples were of the belief that it was the done thing to stay together for the sake of the children, because marriage was a sacrament and it was against the law of God to leave. Economic pressure existed particularly for women because most had no financial resources by which to live if they left a relationship. For many people then, marriage was as much an institutional arrangement as a way of relating. More specifically, the function of marriage was to provide a context for rearing children, and the division of roles gave the man the responsibility for financial support and the woman the responsibility for home-making and childcare. The primary goal was survival and the expectations of the people in marriages were low. All that changed in the decades since the 1950s. The function of marriage changed radically as a result of two important developments: widespread use of contraceptives, and economic progress that ensured higher standards of living for less work. Within a relatively short time people in general changed their focus in marriage away from survival and childbearing to personal fulfilment. I believe that the vast majority of marriages until then were, for the most part, functional arrangements. The love between partners was often a practical one, most did not communicate at any deep level, and unhappiness was widely tolerated. Those who had time to cultivate romance, to spend reasonable time together without being exhausted were the elite.

The change of priorities to wanting the relationship to fulfil one's needs and to be a source of happiness brought great pressure to bear on relationships, and still does. It became economically possible for people to separate and the power of religious authority to prevent such changes was gradually weakened by the progressive secularisation of Western society. As a consequence most marriages in the United States end in divorce and we in Europe are following suit. We are looking to a time when the concept of marriage as a lifelong relationship is no longer a sustainable ideal. The end of the nuclear family is at hand and we have no real alternative to replace it as yet. All these changes have particular relevance for the pursuit of intimacy.

We cannot turn back the wheel of time, and we should not, for there is little to be said for living out one's life in an unhappy relationship. As the years go by I become more and more convinced that unhappiness in a marriage is one of the greatest types of chronic suffering a person can go through. The constant pressure to cope with someone you no longer love, or sometimes even like, the loss of the potential and possibility for companionship and love, the surrender of one's sexual and emotional needs are all akin to an erosion of the soul. Those in the world of therapy who blithely say that happiness is within you and one should be able to be content and happy in all situations are in this regard talking nonsense. It is, in my opinion, almost impossible to experience a good quality of life and happiness while continuing in an unhappy relationship. It is further a cause of great stress and emotional sickness.

So then the expectations for intimacy, for marriage as a source of happiness and fulfilment have all come centre stage. And as a result large numbers of marriages are breaking up. In most cases there is a belief by those leaving their relationships that they might find what they are looking for elsewhere. While the research on this subject suggests that many are modestly successful (some simply because their expectations have decreased second time around), there is plenty of evidence to suggest that intimacy is elusive.

What do I mean by intimacy? One writer suggests that we can use the phonetics of the word as a starting point — intimacy is in-to-me-see. Intimacy is about being seen, being known at the deepest level of one's being, it is about connecting at a soul level to another, its essence is contained in the Judaeo-Christian notion of a man and woman becoming one. By this I do not mean a codependent relationship where people lose their identity, rather I am referring to the bringing together of two unique souls, combining their male and female energies, leaving both enriched and confirmed in their own identity. I believe that this form of relationship is quite rare. In order to have an intimate relationship a person must have a lot of maturity of their own. All relationships are a product of the people in them. Thus some relationships can never become intimate by virtue of the people in them. My close friend Norman gave me an insight from John Donne's poetry that reflects this truth.

My face in thine eye, thine in mine appears,
And true plaine hearts doe in the faces rest,
Where can we finde two better hemispheares
Without sharpe North, without declining West?
What ever dyes, was not mixt equally;
If our two loves be one, or, thou and I
Love so alike, that none doe slacken, none can die.

The key line in this verse is 'What ever dyes, was not mixt equally'. Based on the ancient art of alchemy we have a deep truth about intimacy. It must be based on equality and an equal mix. To me this means that intimacy is available to those who are at the same level of spiritual and emotional development who can treat each other as true equals.

Some relationships cannot become intimate even if those in them have the qualities to bring this gift to the relationship. This occurs when the people in the relationship have hurt each other too much. Ironically, those that have a great potential for intimacy also tend to have high expectations and sometimes a passionate reaction to the failure of the relationship to provide their intimacy needs. In reaction to these losses the people can do so much damage to each other emotionally that the relationship is too badly injured to recover. In my work this is often the most tragic kind of event. To help people who are unsuited to each other find a dignified way to part is less difficult than to see people who could have had something beautiful end their relationship because the wounds were too deep, and it would take too long for them to heal. With these realities in mind we can now discuss some of the common blocks to intimacy that face men in relationship to their partners.

Affection

We have seen in chapter 13 that many men find it difficult to be affectionate and tend to seek their affection needs through sex. This is because the role of touch has not been properly developed in their early lives. This often leaves the partner frustrated and upset because the complaint is that her man is affectionate only when he wants sex, or similarly, he can never just leave it at affection; I hear this sort of thing so often: 'Sometimes I just want a hug, and now I refuse to respond because I know that if we hug he is just going to want to go further.' Being affectionate often means making a decision to give your partner a kiss just for the sake of it. It means sneaking up behind her and putting your arms around her and nuzzling the back of her neck, and then just leaving it at that. For some men this is simply a matter of realising that this is part of the practice of nurturing a relationship. If you are waiting until you feel like doing it you might end up never getting there.

Nourishing and cultivating a relationship is not very different in principle from nourishing and cultivating any living thing. It means giving it what it needs to grow. Any gardener realises that sometimes he doesn't feel like weeding or spraying or digging, but if he wants a blooming display by summer he needs to give this kind of commitment. Being affectionate is part of nourishing human love. The fact that it is often a damaged part of men's lives does not take away its central importance.

Obviously, if a relationship has been starved of affection for years then it is important to go carefully in this area. Very small subtle expressions are possible. Gently touching an arm during a conversation, stroking the hair briefly when giving a peck on the cheek when parting are useful ways to start the process. Very gradually, these expressions will deepen and evoke a positive response in return. Men who wish to learn the art of rebuilding intimacy must practise the art of subtle affection for its own sake rather than as a prelude to sex. I am assuming here that the relationship is still a loving one. Some relationships, as I have said earlier, are irredeemable.

Communication

A second block to intimacy is difficulty communicating. Once again it is important to set out some qualifying remarks about communication. There are some relationships that will, at best, grow into a reasonably secure and functionally successful arrangement. Communication skills can help these relationships to avoid some of the more damaging types of pitfalls. Other relationships will not survive in any decent sort of way no matter what kind of communication skills are learned; these are relationships that should never have been started. And then there are some relationships that have the potential to fulfil the dream of a lifelong partnership that is satisfying and enriching to the people in it. Communication skills are therefore not a panacea for success in relationships. They are necessary but not always sufficient to guarantee intimacy.

With these comments setting some of the limitations to the effectiveness of better communication, there are several key areas that men, in general, can improve in their relationship with their partners. These have been explored in some detail in John Gray's work *Men are from Mars, Women are from Venus* and *What Your Mother Couldn't Tell You and Your Father Didn't Know*, and other books such as *Why Do Women Write More Letters than They Post?* and *Why Men Don't Listen and Women Don't Read Maps*. These books have a central theme that argues that men are not naturally prepared for the kind of communication women want. We have seen earlier in this book that men, from the earliest years, are conditioned to suppress vulnerability, to have inappropriate reaction to pain, to have diminished levels of intimacy and to have limited use for language. John Gray and others develop these themes and show the kinds of ways that men fail in relationships with women because of their difficulties in communication. I have one grave reservation about some of this work.

These books are very useful as a *description* of the way that men have difficulty with communication. I believe that they are seriously flawed in their tacit assumption that men's difficulties with communication are in some way an intrinsic part of being male, rather than, as I see it, a dysfunctional state learned and cultivated over the centuries. Consequently, these books suggest that women must come to understand and accept these limitations, and relate to men through this dysfunction. I think this is short-sighted and naive. I am inclined to agree with psychotherapist and author Frank Pittman when he advises a young man to avoid John Gray like the plague, saying 'he offers a formula for male loneliness and female frustration'. While not being quite as negative I think men should read what Gray has to say in terms of describing their difficulties but need to look elsewhere in getting beyond them.

To condense most of what these books come up with about male communication, there are four abilities that men need to develop: (i) the skills of reflective listening, (ii) learning not to see everything as a problem to be solved, (iii) being honest about when you wish not to talk, and (iv) the skill of direct self-reflected statements.

Reflective listening is a type of listening that helps men to develop empathy. Empathy, we have seen earlier, is a key element in forming emotional bonds with others and is trained out of young boys early in life. Reflective listening is about listening so as to understand what the other person is trying to communicate, with particular emphasis on their emotional state. A classic example of reflective listening is the response, 'You seem to be angry, hurt, frustrated (or whatever the emotion appears to be) about this.' The person in this situation responds to the feelings being expressed rather than to the details contained in the verbal message. Many men would be surprised at just how little they can read in their partner once they begin to use this kind of listening.

This kind of communication is often difficult for men, who are more inclined to focus on the verbal message and to see if it is making sense, is logical, and if they can find a way to solve the difficulty embedded in the verbal message. Men are inclined to be literal-minded and believe a verbal message such as 'I'm fine' when every other aspect of the person tells them that this is not the case. Listening for emotions rather than to words is a key beginning point in effective communication between partners. Once the feelings have been recognised this can open up another avenue where men can improve, namely how they deal with another's emotional state.

Men have, in general, been conditioned to solve problems. The focus on achievement on the one hand and the protective urge on the other leaves many with a limited capacity to tolerate a situation when their loved one is troubled or in difficulty. Common reactions vary from coming up with gloriously inept solutions to complex problems, to patronising dismissals. The first key area of improvement here involves the acceptance that it is not a man's job to solve a woman's problem unless he is specifically asked to do so. Secondly, he needs to respect his partner's ability to solve her own difficulties. He may be of some assistance sometimes by talking it over, sometimes by asking if there is anything he can do to help, and other times by just having a listening ear as she clarifies for herself what she wishes to do. Any of these three approaches is much better than offering an ill-thought-out and perhaps completely irrelevant suggestion for something that in the end is often none of his business.

Honesty about when he is available for communication is difficult but in the end a much better policy. Indirect messages that shut off communication are deeply upsetting and sometimes insulting. Using the newspaper as a shield or the television as a distraction from the person who is trying to communicate are some typical ways that some men try to avoid talking to their partners. These have to be relinquished by those who wish to pursue the path of intimacy. Direct communication means being brave enough to tell someone that you don't feel like talking and that you want to switch off by watching television for a while, or reading, or going for a walk. There is an extremely important difference between using these activities for recreation and explaining your need for them, and using them as a way of escaping responsibility to be honest with a loved one. The latter hurts and in the end drives a wedge between the couple.

Another way in which men in general can improve their communication with their spouse is to speak directly in terms of what is going on for them. This means learning to begin sentences with the words 'I feel' and 'I think'. Abstract generalisations on the one hand and 'You' statements on the other either lead to a state of confusion as to what is going on or put the recipient on the defensive. It seems so simple to think of communication about oneself as being three distinct stages: one, looking inside oneself; two, identifying an emotional reaction or a belief/opinion about something; and three, simply saying what it is. And yet this simple three-stage process can become so complicated and confused. A great source of this confusion lies in the next area of difficulty, that of unrealistic expectations.

Unrealistic expectations

One of the greatest sources of conflict in relationships is the progression from the state of being in love, to the stage of realistic loving. The being in love stage is for the most part an illusion. It is perhaps what ensures the survival of the human race because it involves extraordinarily powerful emotions that seem at the time to be unstoppable. When you fall in love you are overwhelmed, one writer calls it 'a divine madness'. It is obsessional, intense and powerfully enslaving. Physically, the hormones and neurotransmitters are transforming even the most sane and pragmatic types into a state of euphoric bliss and intense anguish. Psychology has gone a long way to help understand what is happening in these altered states of consciousness, to such an extent that Irvin Yalom coined the wonderfully poignant phrase 'love's executioner' to describe the way that therapeutic psychology has unveiled the illusions and denials that go to make up that incredible feeling of 'being in love'.

By its nature the 'being in love' experience is addictive, as well as being blinding. And many people do not learn that the 'being in love' state is a stage, an important yet rather immature one that helps to get them to bond with another long enough to build a different kind of love. Those who cannot journey from the 'being in love' state to the loving state end up disillusioned, angry and often punitive towards their lover. They may leave the relationship and seek out a new 'in love' experience, not realising that it is a preparatory stage for a long-term relationship. This does not mean that all people who fall in love with each other are suited to a long-term relationship, nor does it mean that those who get to a sustaining loving relationship have to go through the 'in love' stage. The point being made here is that most people who go through an in love experience must move into a different form of love if the relationship is to be sustained.

Some people don't know this and live with a constant sense of loss. In order to move from an in love state to a sustaining love relationship there are certain crucial elements that the couple must share. These are examined in *Healing Life's Hurts* so I won't repeat the content here.

Men need to learn how to survive what Michael Gurian calls 'the descent into disillusionment' stage of a relationship without reverting to the two more common male reactions — closing down and emotional withdrawal. Men usually cannot cope with the deep hurt produced by their sense of loss in a way that leaves the relationship still working. Many men have lived their whole lives in a fruitless and barren relationship because they did not know how to stay emotionally available in trying to sort out the conflict that is at the heart of the transition from the in love stage to the mature loving stage. Their spouses too suffered enormous and chronic pain as the men they loved disappeared into some unreachable place. Many remained faithful, honest and helpful in many ways but the emotional bond was broken and beyond salvage. The great challenge to men is to learn that hurt can be surmounted and the road to intimacy requires coming back into communion again and again, until understanding and healing is found. A lot, of course, depends on the spouse also and this is where Donne's insight is most relevant. Equally mixt means equally committed, equally passionate to save love and to reach understanding.

Summary

Most men have deep needs for affectionate sexual love but often sabotage themselves and their partners because of fear and unfamiliarity with the landscape of intimacy. This chapter has examined some of the central elements involved in developing and cultivating intimate and satisfying relationships between men and women. Its focus has been on the need for men to realise that they need to develop better communication skills. They need to rely less on trying to solve relationship problems and focus more on listening for understanding. They need to risk vulnerability, rather than trying to control everything, and they need to make the pursuit and expression of love a priority over the need to be right.

15 Rebuilding Fatherhood

Introduction

It is an unfortunate consequence of dismantling patriarchy that fatherhood as a vocation and central element in the healthy human family has been damaged. Patriarchy is the term used by the women's movement to describe the oppression of women economically, intellectually, emotionally and spiritually. Patriarchy is built on the assumption that men are superior to women and patriarchal societies emerge when the structures of a society are constructed to maintain this prejudice by disempowering women. Patriarchy as a social system has had a long career and continues to a greater or lesser extent in most societies. It is a worthwhile and valuable goal that it be dismantled. Nowadays, however, the lines between fatherhood and patriarchy are less easily seen because any fathering type of behaviour can so easily be assumed to be part of that prejudicial bias against women that men of goodwill and evolved thinking would seek to undo.

Consequently, fatherhood suffers from a loss of place. This is easily seen in the reflection of fatherhood on popular television. The dumbing down of dad seems to be an important theme. In programmes from *The Simpsons* to *King of the Hill* (one has to admire the cynical twist of the title) and from *Married — with Children* to *Roseanne*, we see fathers as caricatures. Generally overweight, rather stupid, out of touch and naive, these fathers lack any qualities that would evoke respect or admiration. Some say that art reflects reality and in this regard our own social structures seem to suggest that fatherhood is of little importance. There are grave imbalances in both the justice system and the employment system in this country where the rights of fathers are concerned.

Despite some of the vitriolic and inaccurate thinking among some feminist writers, a society without fathers is, in my opinion, in deep trouble. As Robert Bly observes, when social forces develop that institutionalise the absence of father, then quite quickly motherhood is lost also. We are, in his view, gradually moving towards a society that is run by 'orphaned adolescents'. And the outcome of this is that both ends of the human family, the young and the old, are disregarded. If we are to reverse this trend we need to examine how to become the kinds of fathers that lead and enrich the world we live in.

Fatherhood

What is fatherhood? There are two elements that need to be clarified here. The state of fatherhood and the process of fathering. A useful analogy to my mind is that of Roman Catholicism. The vast majority of people born in this country until recently would be baptised into the church at six weeks old. They had no choice in the matter. Thus they were Roman Catholics. Being Roman Catholic in this country means absolutely nothing in terms of religious practice or moral behaviour. One could be an atheist and a Roman Catholic (and there are plenty of those around). It is difficult to leave the church and become a non-Catholic. As Pat Conroy says wittily in *Beach Music*, becoming a non-Catholic is as difficult as becoming a non-Oriental. Being a father is akin to being a Catholic. It is a state whereby a man's female partner has borne a child which she conceived by him. Even if he leaves and spends the rest of his life without any contact he is still a father. If he stays he could be a good father or a bad father. And I am firmly of the view that bad fathering is not better than no fathering. Bad fathering often prevents the contribution of other father figures who could bring good influences to bear. The process of fathering is about the kinds of behaviours that make for good fathers. This chapter is concerned with this second element, the process of fathering.

The process of fathering

I believe that fathering is a part of mature masculinity and does not require having children of one's own. It is an attitude to one's place in the world, and one's task in life. We can see this point much more clearly if we compare it with how we see the role of mothering. Our attitudes to motherhood are clear reminders that mothering is not simply about having and caring for children. Mother Teresa had no children of her own but she became a good mother to millions of suffering people, both directly in her day-to-day work, and indirectly through her help of the other 'mothers' that she trained and influenced. A friend of mine who worked with her told me a story that so well illustrated her mothering of the lost and disenfranchised. On arriving in Calcutta my friend was chosen by Mother Teresa to help in one of her centres for the dying. Mother Teresa told her that the deepest message that gives one the strength to do this work is to see Jesus in each individual, no matter how bad a condition that person is in. Intellectually understanding this is one thing but actually experiencing it is another. Very soon it was to be tested. A man was brought to my friend. He was beyond medical help and was going to die. My friend's task was to prepare him to die with dignity. This meant cleaning and bathing his sores. She proceeded to work for hours with a tweezers picking the thousands of maggots from this man's massive infections, cleaning, bathing and bandaging. Just as she finished, this man looked at her through his anguish and awful pain, gave her a sweet and knowing smile and died. For that time my friend became this man's mother. The world is littered with millions of such instances. We have no problem in recognising this form of mothering in the world. And it is no different for fathering.

Fathering is about vision, direction, guidance and encouragement. The growing men's movement has placed much focus on the notion of mentoring. This is about men becoming mentors, wise and mature guides for other younger men. I think this is a very useful development but I would prefer to see this as simply one aspect of a renewal and reconstruction of men as fathers in the wider context of the world we live in. What kind of fathering is it for mature men in the media to engage in ridiculous freak shows that elevate the banal and sordid chaos of some people's lives into entertainment? What kind of fathering are mature men engaged in when they work for a gutter press that destroys the fabric of people's personal lives just to sell a few more papers? What kind of fathering are mature men involved in when they disenfranchise fathers through the court system? Every man is a father, whether he does it well or not will shape the future of our world. I am blessed because of several men who became fathers at critical periods in my life from childhood into early adulthood. Good fathers see the spark of talent, the special something in others. Like Michelangelo who saw the statue of David in the lump of marble before he even touched it with a chisel, fathers 'see' often what the person themselves cannot see. Bad fathering is about using this potential for one's own ends, or simply ignoring it or trying to destroy it. Bad fathering is competitive, it is afraid to let another shine. It is mean and small-minded. Many people get into positions of authority, take on the fathering role and then misuse it to their own ends.

It is one thing to see something special in others, it is another to help them to express it. This sometimes means teaching discipline and endurance. There is no such thing as a frce lunch and the character we try to help others develop takes time, patience and commitment. Fathers stick with those they assist; through praise, confrontation, holding firm, they provide a person with a sense of confidence. When you are believed in by someone you respect, you begin to believe in yourself.

Fathering is also about imparting skills, teaching something to another. It is one of the grave difficulties that inhere in much of society that the fathering role of teaching is becoming lost. I think this has something to do with the collapse of authority. Again much of the authoritarianism of the past was cruel and demeaning and it is right that it should be dismantled, but what do we put in its place? Where is the wisdom for running the world going to come from? I don't think that the lowest common denominator of wisdom, or the majority vote in matters that require knowledge and depth, will guide us into the next millennium. We need people who are mature, women who will be good mothers to the world and men who will be good fathers.

Thus far I have looked at fatherhood in general terms as an attitude towards the world that is part of mature masculinity. The core of this chapter is, however, examining the more common meaning of fathering, the role of the man in the care and development of his children.

Fathering within the family

Before discussing ways that fathers can deepen and strengthen their bonds with their children there is an important warning to be made. Hillman's acorn presents this warning with eloquence and power. He says:

> when your child becomes the reason for your life, you have abandoned the invisible reason you are here . . . Any father who has abandoned the small voice of his unique genius, turning it over to the small child he has fathered, cannot bear the reminders of what he has neglected. He cannot tolerate the idealism that arises so naturally and spontaneously in the child, the romantic enthusiasm, the sense of fairness, the clear-eyed beauty, the attachment to

> little things and the interest in the big questions. All of this becomes unbearable to the man who has forgotten his daimon. Instead of learning from the child, who is living evidence of the invisibles in everyone's life, the father capitulates to the child, disturbing its growing down into civilisation by setting it up in a toy world. Result — a child-dominated fatherless culture with dysfunctional children with pistol packing power.

Being a father is a role a man takes in the life of his children, it cannot take the place of his calling and if it does he will grow to resent his children. This is something that is neglected in much of the focus of modern parenting psychology. That focus has nowhere been as popularised as in the United States, a nation that despite such widespread child-centred ideology has an appalling record of neglect of its children.

Related to this error is the father neglect where work is concerned. Robert Bly in the book *Iron John* makes the important point that much father neglect is the result of men having to leave their home to work in places where their children cannot see them. This is a relatively new phenomenon and is a direct result of the Industrial Revolution. Thus:

> when a father, absent during the day, returns home at six, his children receive only his temperament, and not his teaching. If the father is working for a corporation, what is there to teach? He is reluctant to tell his son what is really going on. The fragmentation of decision making in corporate life, the massive effort that produces the corporate willingness to destroy the environment for the sake of profit, the prudence, even cowardice, that one learns in bureaucracy — who wants to teach that? . . . What the father brings home today is usually a touchy mood springing from powerlessness and despair mingled with long-standing shame and the numbness peculiar to those who hate their jobs.

When we bring these two related pieces together we get a picture of an alienated, emasculated and tired man who cannot convert himself into the kind of father his children need. That is why much of what has been discussed in chapters 10 and 11 is central to improving the personhood of the man and has direct bearing on his role as an effective father. When this work is being done, a man changes. He becomes more self-aware, less devastated by the demands of work and his sense of being lost, thus he has more energy to devote to the specifics of good fathering. Without doing this self-development work most men have just another burden of failure to carry, that of being a bad father. To quote Hillman again:

> Present in body and absent in spirit he lies back on the couch, shamed by his own daimon for the potentials in his soul that will not be subdued. He feels himself inwardly subversive, imagining in his passivity extremes of aggression and desire that must be suppressed. Solution: more work, more money, more drink, more weight, more things, more infotainment, and an almost fanatic dedication of his mature male life to the kids so that they can grow up straight and straight up the consumer ladder in the pursuit of their own happiness.

And all of this is done without any real relationship, no soul building and no true connection. The process of good fathering starts with becoming a healthier man. Several key elements in this process have already been discussed, here we need to turn our attention to some of the specific aspects of enriching and developing the art of fathering.

The art of fathering

Recently, I had the opportunity to speak at a certification event where people were being awarded certificates for completing a parenting course. This course was organised and sponsored by the organisation Accord, which is affiliated to the Catholic church. It comprises three modules, each dealing with different age groups from early childhood up to late adolescence. The course is presented in a group seminar format where people interact with facilitators in the challenge and process of learning. I was very impressed with the quality of the programme and the materials provided. On the strength of this I agreed to attend the completion ceremony, where the local bishop presented the awards. What struck me forcibly was that of the one hundred people who did this parenting course, only two were men. I was left wondering why so few? Some obvious answers are that it was run by the church, so maybe that put some men off, maybe the night didn't suit others, some men are shy about courses such as this. But even taking these and other variables into account, the enormous disparity can only be evidence that men do not see the need to learn how to become better fathers or would not engage in a course of instruction to do so. Either way men are seriously at a loss in this regard.

What do men believe about their role as father? In a time of such chaos and difficulty among many young people, where crime, drug abuse and teenage suicide are at an all-time high, how can men deny that some of this has to do with the role of fathering? Are men in denial about the needs of children, or are they simply lost and confused? Have the distance and difficulties with their own fathers left them without any insight into the responsibility and duty to excellence in this most important role? I don't know the answer to these questions. What I do know is that most men can benefit from help in developing as fathers. The remainder of this book could be written on the topic and still not do as good a job as one of the courses on parenting that are available. That so few men are yet ready to seek instruction and help in learning about healthy fatherhood is a source of great concern for those who see the implication for society at large. This book cannot redress this situation. What it may offer is some brief contribution to helping men who wish to improve their skills as fathers.

The discussion here is limited to three very practical and easy to implement guidelines that can improve father-child relationships at any age. These are (i) eye contact, (ii) focused attention and (iii) physical affection. Improving these communication skills helps men to relate better to children (and to others as well) and can help debunk the rather fashionable caricatures of fathers as either emotionally retarded autocrats or incompetent, inarticulate slobs. These suggestions are not a replacement for more in-depth opportunities to learn about oneself as father and the needs and developmental issues of childhood. They are, however, very useful and practical ways to begin improving in this crucial aspect of male responsibility.

Eye contact

Eye contact is one of the most powerful non-verbal signals that communicates a great deal about our feelings and attitude to any event that is happening between two people. Unfortunately, eye contact is used far more as a form of expressing anger than love. Fathers have almost no difficulty in using eye contact to communicate feelings of anger and domination. There is a great example of negative eye contact in the animal kingdom. I call this the silverback gorilla reaction. Gorillas are very peace-loving social creatures. Each family group comprises males and females, young and old, who live harmoniously together and are led by a patriarchal older male. Every now and then the peace of the group is broken when that male is threatened in some way, or suffers some slight, imagined or otherwise. He erupts in rage, screams and shouts, beats his breast and glares at some unfortunate member of the group, often a younger male who poses some form of threat. There is rarely any injury and most of it is show. But watching this event on film reminds one of the many similarities it has to the interaction between some fathers and their families. Sitting quietly in the corner behind a newspaper or avidly watching the fifth rerun of the same news broadcast, the 'silverback' human male sometimes erupts in a similar fashion. In this event there is no problem making eye contact, and the message is very clear. Don't **** with me.

Most fathers can improve their connection with their children by extending the use of this very effective non-verbal technique. Many fathers are for example less comfortable in using eye contact in communicating interest, warmth and love. This is particularly true in their dealings with adolescent children and more especially boys. And most of this is quite unconscious. By staying aware of eye contact during communication a father can enrich his relationship. Many fathers do not make eye contact when they greet their children in the morning, after work or saying goodnight. Often engrossed in something else, they assume that verbal interaction will suffice. All the research evidence on communication tells us that this is not the case. Non-verbal signals themselves are far more important and influential in their effects on relationships than are verbal. And eye contact is the non-verbal signal par excellence. Closely related, however, is the element of focused attention.

Focused attention

It is a common theme in most of the recent books that explore the differences between the sexes that men can really do only one thing at a time, whereas women are able to deal with many. Stereotypical examples abound. A woman can talk with a friend on the phone while making up food for a child, writing some reminder notes and pencilling in appointments in her diary. A man on the other hand answers the phone, gets distracted by the conversation, lets the milk boil over, loses his pencil and ends up angry. While this cameo exaggerates the issue, it seems true to say that men seem to work best when able to give their complete attention to individual tasks. This is perhaps what has allowed them to push forward so many of the positive achievements and breakthroughs in science, medicine, technology, art and music. And to fail so miserably in the area of relationships. I have no doubt that similar achievements would accrue if women had the opportunities to give the same focused and singular attention to these areas. It is not simply a matter of talent, it is also about devotion, commitment and single-mindedness. Men, historically at least, seem to have developed these qualities in the areas of achievement, but have not yet learned to use them regularly in the area of relationships.

More specifically, many fathers do not give focused attention to their children. Their communication and interactions are often tangential to other activities. A child is more likely to get focused attention if he or she is in trouble. A school report that shows failure in several subjects is likely to get more attention, longer time spent in discussion, and more eye contact, more questions and comment than is one that shows excellence. Why is this? Again the notion of men as problem solvers comes to the fore. When a child does well in school most fathers will give a compliment, and perhaps some word of encouragement such as 'keep it up', and sometimes, unfortunately, some silly motivational spiel about doing better next time. The whole thing lasts ten seconds. There is no problem being solved because most fathers do not see the quality of their relationship as something that needs continuous attention. The negative report is a problem and therefore enters a different category of male thinking — the problem solving area. When this area is engaged, a whole plethora of communication systems opens up: the lecture, the historical reminiscing about how hard it was back in the old days, the motivational spin, the threat, some advice on how to improve, and finally, perhaps, a kind word to soften the edge of it all. For most, that is the end of the issue until the next report, and the interim months of dealing with school and learning are given little attention.

I am being somewhat hard on men here. These generalisations are an effort to highlight a difficulty that many fathers encounter — how to give children focused and special attention when there are no problems to be solved. If fathers learned how to do so there would be fewer problems around. Men are experts at focused attention, they just don't apply it to their children. When a man realises this lack, he has most of the skills required to address it. It means applying the same thoroughness that is given to listening to the news, fixing a leaking tap, building a software program, improving his golf swing, to his relationship with his children. How often does a father listen with the same rapt attention and single-mindedness to his child recounting an incident in school, as he does to the story of collapsing stock values in Tokyo, or an earthquake in Afghanistan!

This may seem somewhat crazy to those who romanticise the issue of child rearing. Some believe that it all should happen naturally, and perhaps they are right. Currently, however, it does not happen naturally for most men. They have for the most part been reared in a way that leaves them struggling in the realm of relating to others, especially to their children. Most fathers would give all for their children, but their concept of what this means needs to change. It is tragic to talk to so many men who worked hard all their lives in a singular devotion to providing well for their children, to give them a better start in life than they themselves had, to find that getting older reveals almost no relationship with their now adult children, who are often angry with them for having been so distant. These men did not lack in devotion, concern or love. They did lack in their ability to regularly turn away from the tasks at hand and towards their children.

A recent conversation with a client comes to mind. Brian, a forty-year-old executive, made a significant change in his life after several months in counselling. He decided that his work, while important, could not replace the value he placed on his family. He refused a promotion that entailed moving to a different city on the grounds that it would have caused great distress to his wife, and a lot of disturbance for his young children. This decision effectively put an end to his career advancement prospects. Pleased with his decision and learning for the first time some crucial aspects of building better relationships, he seemed quite resolved about his choices.

Two months later Brian booked an appointment. He was struggling with some regret and confusion. As the session continued it emerged that much of Brian's choice about his family was based on a principle and that the actual living out of the decision was another matter entirely. He was irritated and frustrated with his children a lot of the time. When we discussed this it became clear that he did not see the role of fatherhood as a specific task. At some level, Brian believed that the relationships would happen automatically without any purposeful intention or activity on his part. He was trying to live as if he were not a father, now without the distraction of long periods away from the family. Thus his children's needs and demands seemed to be intrusions to which he reacted with frustration and anger. He had to understand that the choice to elect his family before his career meant that now he had to learn a set of skills and work hard at a new role, that of fatherhood. He could see clearly that his career success to date had been based on being skilful, committed and enthusiastic about the job. He now needed to apply these elements to his job as father.

Physical affection

That children need physical affection is just common sense. Most so-called 'primitive' and 'simple' tribes and societies exhibit high levels of affection for children throughout childhood. The more technologically advanced societies are the ones that seem to have some trouble in this area. Psychology, a relatively recent science in terms of human history, has only formulated explanations for why affection is so important. Societies who have no exposure to these explanations seem to do very well without them.

Physical affection is an absolute requirement for healthy child development. There are several reasons for this. Physical affection is a crucial element in building emotional bonds and these are central to emotional development, the ability to feel, to relate and to experience intimacy. Physical affection is also important for physical health. Rene Spitz's work in the 1950s revolutionised our understanding of the relationship between touch and health in infancy. Children's hospitals that had very high levels of commitment to hygiene and clinical efficiency, and as a result reduced the amount of handling experienced by the babies, had higher levels of infant mortality and illness than did those less careful institutions which handled children more. Spitz began to identify the 'failure to thrive syndrome' in those children who did not receive enough affection.

More recent advances tell us that the power of touch has great healing qualities not just in childhood but throughout life. Fascinating developments in pet therapy are currently under way. Seriously ill children who have pets such as rabbits, cats and dogs made available to them appear to react better to medications and to have faster recovery periods. Studies reveal that older people who live without a partner are more likely to live longer and to suffer less disease if they have a pet for company than if they do not. Pets in general fulfil two needs, companionship and affection. Here we are interested in the power of affection. Affection functions by reducing levels of anxiety, increasing feelings of security, stimulating certain brain chemicals called endorphins that seem directly related to the immune system. All this information tells us that human beings need lots of affection.

Unfortunately, it is also known that people who have been bereft of affection in early life can struggle greatly with it as adults. Monkeys and dogs that are deprived of touch as infants can have immense difficulty in managing their own young as adults. The reader may remember the discussion of brain development in chapter 1. These animal studies suggest that at least in the animal kingdom early exposure to maternal affection lays down the brain pathways for later abilities to nurture young. How people relate to affection then seems to be also profoundly affected by experience.

Fatherly affection

Becoming more affectionate is a challenge for some fathers. Many find that affection with babies and young children is relatively easy. Sometimes lack of expression of affection with this age group is simply a matter of oversight on the part of the father. He may fail to realise just how important it is and how good it feels for the child to receive that spontaneous hug, or that reassuring tousling of the hair or stroke on the cheek. Some fathers are of the mistaken belief that providing affection is the role and responsibility of mother. Once a father who is relatively at ease with affection realises that it is important to become purposeful in delivering affection to children, rather than relying on spontaneity alone (I am not suggesting some robotic dutiful task here), there can be pleasant improvements for all concerned.

Some fathers, however, have greater difficulties with being affectionate. They may have suffered a lack of affection when they were little boys and now are in some difficulty with their own children. They may be afraid that overt displays of affection, especially with their sons, are signs of femininity, weakness or homosexuality. Consequently, some may maintain a distance from any signs or displays of affection, and thus impoverish their relationships with their children. Other, more naturally affectionate fathers, who restrain their expressions out of fear or mistaken beliefs, may limit themselves to 'manly' displays — the friendly punch on the shoulder, a spontaneous wrestling match or some other sort of horseplay. These in themselves are helpful because they fulfil one of the key roles of affection, that of building and maintaining emotional bonds. They are severely limited in other areas, however, such as communicating specific emotions like concern or empathy, reassuring an anxious child or troubled adolescent, or communicating support. Additionally, such displays, when they are the only means of being affectionate, teach young boys to become uncomfortable with being affectionate to other men.

Fathers who have trouble in the realm of expressing affection also tend to be unable to receive it. And thus they miss out on one of life's great pleasures, the spontaneous hugs, tender touch and embraces of those they love. Making changes in these areas is difficult but worth the effort. A first step is to realise that affection in all its forms is a good thing. A second is to realise that to deprive one's children of affection is a form of neglect. These two beliefs often give the motivation for change. And we know from all that has been said so far that when men see a good reason for doing something they can give a great deal of commitment and endurance to bringing it to fruition.

Affection, like focused attention, can be made a priority in interacting with a child. At early stages this may seem a bit uncomfortable for a father who is somewhat more distant, but it does get easier and eventually becomes automatic. It is most helpful to begin with very subtle and easy to deliver forms of expression. The key here is for both father and child to feel safe during the interaction. The hand on the shoulder or the hand placed between the shoulder blades when a child is sitting focused on some task is very unthreatening because the other non-verbal channels of communication are not in play, eye contact is diverted away to the task, and body posture is also oriented towards the task. When this kind of affection becomes a regular feature, the next type could be the hand on the arm when speaking directly to a child or adolescent. This is quite powerful, but still not so close as to cause discomfort. Gradually, the amount of gentle physical contact increases until a point is reached when even men who had a lot of difficulty in this area can hug their children without any inner conflict. Of course, the children may have become so used to having no physical affection from their dad that they may have trouble with it. Subtlety and patience and not being invasive are the key elements in making these changes.

Summary

This chapter has examined the area of men as fathers. Generation after generation of men are called on to achieve, to compete and to succeed. Very few awards are given for their ability to be good fathers. If anything, men are discouraged from investing themselves in this role if it means reducing the time and energy available to the tasks of accumulation and winning. And yet there is no finer calling than to offer one's own special wisdom and leadership to those growing up in our care. To love effectively, to guide and teach, and to see the young man or woman emerge in response to good fathering is a rich blessing. And one that will last far longer than faded certificates or crystal decanters.

16 Further Reflections and Conclusion

Introduction

In the introduction to this book I said that men still rule the world and that the world shows the results. Fritjof Capra summarises the elements of this influence. He says, in *The Tao of Physics*, that we have 'favoured self-assertion over integration, analysis over synthesis, rational knowledge over intuitive wisdom, science over religion, competition over cooperation, expansion over conservation, and so on. This one-sided development has now reached a highly alarming stage; a crisis of social, ecological, moral and spiritual dimensions.'

Thus far, this book has examined central aspects of how men function in such a world as well as the areas of difficulties they encounter. It is not exhaustive in its examination, attempting to draw with broad strokes the story of male conditioning, rather than present fine historical or psychological analysis of the subject matter. Consequently, this book is really only a starting point for those who wish to deepen their understanding of men in today's world. That is its primary purpose and I hope I have done it some justice.

There are other important areas that have not been examined except by indirect reference. These are also of great importance in developing a broad picture of masculinity and manhood. Some that seem of particular relevance are those of male violence, the concept of the 'new' man, and getting old. This chapter calls attention to these areas in the expectation that further exploration will be given to them in a later work.

Male violence

No book about men would be complete without some reference to the problem of male violence. According to expert in the field John Archer, 'most human violence is carried out by men. Male violence is clearly a problem in the modern world, and may even be *the* major source of human suffering. It is, however, intractable as it is deep rooted in biology and culture, and is supported by male vested interests of many kinds.' Before exploring this issue it is important to note that most men are not violent. It is not, therefore, inherent to being male to be violent.

While it may seem intractable and even perhaps impossible to eliminate, we must continue to find ways to prevent the spread of violence, and to treat its perpetrators effectively. Such a task is far beyond the reach of this book, and I will limit this discussion to some reflections that seem relevant to the issue. A useful starting point is a comment made in a recent interview by Rose-Marie Dousse, a survivor of the 1997 Luxor massacre. After describing the scenes of terror and horror that unfolded that day, when she survived by covering herself in the blood of a man dying beside her, she said:

> Not a day goes by when I do not think of my friend Astrid, who died before my eyes. But when I think of the victims, I eliminate the horrible conditions in which they died. I keep the sorrow. I exclude the fear. I believe this to be a mark of respect to their memory. For me the tragedy of Luxor lies in their deaths. The violence and obscure motives of the assassins has nothing to do with sorrow. It has only to do with the absurdity of the world of men.

And yes, it must appear absurd. How do we explain the mindset of a young Arab who slits the throat of a young woman, a complete stranger, as she pleads for help for her dying mother, and who then dances with joy? If we can reach an understanding of this and other kinds of violence then perhaps we can do something about it.

In my own thinking on the matter I have reached several conclusions. Firstly, the potential for violence exists in all people, men and women, but is more easily activated in men. Men are biologically and psychologically more vulnerable to becoming violent. Again and again history proves this to be the case. The potential for violence can remain dormant for decades but can show its ugly face once certain circumstances arise. This means that potential tormentors, those who could become cold-blooded killers, can have lived out normal lives, done no harm to anyone because the circumstances that would trigger the potential for violence did not arise. Perhaps the clearest exposition of the dark side that lies in human nature is given by Primo Levi, who writes this account in *The Drowned and the Saved*:

> In the gas chamber have been jammed together and murdered the components of a recently arrived convoy and the squad is performing its horrendous everyday work, sorting out the tangle of corpses, washing them with hoses and transporting them to the crematorium, but on the floor they find a young woman who is still alive. The event is exceptional, unique . . . The men are perplexed, death is their trade at all hours . . . but this woman is alive. They hide her, warm her, bring her beef broth, question her, she is sixteen years old . . . She has not understood, but she has seen; therefore she must die, and the men of the squad know it just as they know that they too must die for the same reason. But these slaves, debased by alcohol and the daily slaughter, are transformed; they no longer have before them the anonymous mass, the flood of frightened stunned people coming off the boxcars; they have a person . . . A

> doctor is called, and he revives the girl with an injection: yes, the gas has not had its effect, she will be able to survive, but where and how? Just then Muhsfeld arrives; he is one of the SS men attached to the death installations . . . he decides: no the girl must die. And yet he does not kill her with his own hands; he calls one of his underlings to eliminate her with a blow to the nape of the neck. Now this man Muhsfeld was not a compassionate man . . . He was tried in 1947 in Cracow, sentenced to death and hanged and this was right; but not even he was a monolith. If he had lived in a different environment and epoch, it is likely that he would have behaved like any other common man.

The last sentence in the above account reveals a deep truth about violent behaviour — that we cannot foresee the extent to which any one of us can be corrupted and turned into a monster. This truth is further affirmed in more recent events. Nowhere has this been more clearly seen than in what is rather euphemistically termed ethnic cleansing. The belief that the holocaust was some kind of aberration partly due to the nature of the German psyche has been undermined by recent events in the Balkans. The political, historical and social aspects of these issues are not of particular relevance here. The events do, however, reflect a common theme concerning the nature of violence: the systematic slaughter of innocent people by others, many of whom had lived alongside each other in peace for years.

If then the potential for violence lies in human nature, there must be some differentiation at work that makes some people violent and others not. In my opinion there are key elements that incite or trigger the violent potential in people, and these are far more likely to be part of male make-up and conditioning, thus making men far more likely to be violent. Three elements that I believe are central to the use of violence are lack of attachment, lack of empathy, and belief in violence as a justifiable form of behaviour. Any one of these elements increases the likelihood of violence. When the three work together, as they do in the instances recounted here, there is a potent and dangerous mix.

Lack of attachment

Eminent child psychologist Jerome Kagan shows us that values such as caring, compassion and loving are grounded in an emotional attachment between a child and those who care for him. When we experience love we are more likely to learn how to love. When we know how to love we are less likely to hurt other people. It's that simple. Boys do not have the same focus and emphasis on building attachment bonds in early childhood and are thus as a group more vulnerable to causing injury to others.

One treatment approach for violent men that focuses on this issue of attachment involves pet therapy. While in prison very violent offenders were given a choice of low-maintenance pets such as rabbits, hamsters and the like. For some, their relationship with their pet was the first emotional attachment they ever had. It is hoped, and is probably likely, that once a person experiences such attachment they begin to develop the capacity to attach emotionally to others.

Yet we also know that there are people who love and yet are violent towards those they profess to love. This is a misunderstanding. People who try to injure those they love are in fact confusing love with need. The intense emotional pain that inheres in fear of loss can sometimes lead a person to violence. This is most likely to occur in close relationships, such as with domestic violence. And if we argue that men are more likely to have such abandonment fears given the nature of their upbringing, it is a small step to conclude that men are more needy, more sensitive to loss and more likely to react intensely in response to abandonment. Those men whose capacity for attachment has been damaged are thus more likely to react violently to those they need (often believing it is their love that is at work). A recent film, *Loved*, explores this issue. One of the characters, a woman who lived in a violent relationship for years, eventually, with much help, is able to leave the abusive relationship. She later learns that her ex-partner is even more violent to the new woman in his life and has caused her serious physical injury. Because he never inflicted such injury on her, she interprets this as meaning that he must have loved his new partner more. The film explores the connection between love and violence in depth and with sensitivity and is chilling in its analysis. To accept violation as a reflection of love is as sick and dysfunctional as the belief that violence can be a form of expression of love.

Loving and consistent attachment in childhood is more likely to lead a person to feel secure, and less desperate for love in adulthood. Fear of abandonment and rejection is thus minimised, and the likelihood of violence diminishes. What then of those who would never harm those they love but can violate others? This leads to the second strand in the cable of violence, lack of empathy.

Lack of empathy

We explored the issue of empathy in an earlier chapter. Here the issue is raised in the context of empathy as relating to violence. Part of empathy is identification. It means that we identify with the other, we realise that they are just like us in some important ways. To a large extent it is more difficult for a person to injure another if they have some emotional feeling for that person's plight. If we know how it feels to be hurt and we know the other is hurting and we feel some compassion for them, then we are unlikely to continue causing them pain. One of the interesting treatment approaches in the rehabilitation of violent men, which has shown some measure of success, has been to try to instil this kind of quality into the perpetrators. Rapists who were consistently confronted, while in prison, by women who had been raped began to show remorse and sadness about what they had done. This remorse occurred only when the walls of hatred and bias against women broke down and they began to see the woman as a feeling human being who was suffering deep anguish as a result of rape. Those who maintained the walls of hatred did not respond to the treatment.

Violence is thus more easily perpetrated on those with whom we do not identify. The focus on competition and achievement teaches boys to dismiss the common ground with others, to perceive them as a threat, to suppress feelings of empathy so as to be able to beat the opponent. Terrence Real speaks of his own son in this regard.

> If we are to come to grips with the extent and the power of the pressures brought to bear on our sons, we must understand that masculine socialization, throughout history and in almost all cultures throughout the world, is inextricably bound up with war. The process of 'masculinization' is one potent enough to take my sweet son Alexander, who loves make-up and dresses, whose favorite identity is the magic fairy, and deliver him a decade or so later into a state in which he will be prepared to kill and be killed . . . It is also the conditioning out of empathy that allows leaders to send in the boys to begin with, cloaking the reality of war with metaphors like 'necessary losses' and 'collateral damage'.

The damage to boys' capacity for empathy is further exacerbated by the male inclination for categorisation. People in general are susceptible to categorising others. It is only a small step to seeing one category (the one we are in) as better than another. Thus the divisions of people into groups, German-Jewish, Serb-Croat, Protestant-Catholic, Black-White, can very easily break down the individual's empathy for those in a different group. As we have seen earlier, it is a key element in training young men to kill that these divisions are made. Again, men are more susceptible to such categorisation. Neurologically, men are more prone to put things, including feelings and experiences, into discrete categories. We have discussed earlier the results of neurological studies that show the male brain tending to operate more in discrete ways than the female. While this allows for more single-minded focus on tasks and projects, it also means that men can simplify things, including people, and thus have a greater capacity to learn the kind of prejudice that leads to violence. When we add this to the third strand — the belief that violence is justifiable — we have the basis for genocide.

Violence as acceptable behaviour

Neither damaged emotional attachment nor lack of identification with others in itself produces violent behaviour. Somewhere along the way a person must give themselves permission to violate, attack or injure others. Most people hold firm beliefs and principles as regards what kind of situation will warrant acting in a way that endangers others. For many these will comprise a belief in the need to protect oneself and others. (We have seen above that they may not stand much testing.) Male violence is almost always a distortion of these beliefs. And in most cases men who become violent hold the belief that it is acceptable to hurt others in response to a perceived threat of loss on the one hand, or in order to achieve some gain on the other. This kind of violence is called instrumental violence. It means that violence is seen as an appropriate instrument or tool to achieve some goal or prevent some slight. From the burglar who beats up an old man for his pension (violence used calculatedly for financial gain) to the husband who beats his wife into submission (violence used to gain control and dominance) to the terrorist who bombs a shop (violence used to gain ideological advantage), these forms of violence all share a common theme. The perpetrators believe that they have a right to use violence.

Two groups of men are particularly prone to learning that

violence is a useful tool, and these groups happen to be those most likely to perpetrate violence in adulthood. These are men who witnessed domestic violence as children, and those from impoverished social circumstances who are continually confronted with what they cannot have on the one hand, and on the other with a steady stream of film and television displaying violence that is justified and presented as a virtue. Of the first group Anne Campbell and Steven Muncer write, 'Developmentally, exposure to violence as a child is a powerful precursor of domestic violence in men . . . Boys in violent families acquire an instrumental theory of violence through modelling, vicarious, and, ultimately, direct reinforcement' ('Men and the meaning of violence'). Violence then breeds violence.

It is not politically correct to connect violent behaviour in men with poverty. And yet there seems to be some connection. In his essay 'Male violence: towards an integration', Paul Gilbert provides thoughtful and sound analysis of the social and cultural roots of violence within capitalist economies. He writes:

> Even though there is growing evidence that after a certain point it is not the overall level of resources in a community that is linked with health, crime and violence but the disparities within the community (Wilkinson 1992), this seems to have little impact on shifting us to more egalitarian social structures. Those with power and resources rarely vote (in large enough numbers) to share them.
>
> Thus society splits into the haves, the have-nots, and the have-lots and those who are disadvantaged tend to collapse into more primitive and male-dominated social structures: violence is pronounced in young males at the margins of society . . . These cultural forces are dehumanising and reduce compassionate mechanisms . . . Potentials for mutual nurturance, compassion, sharing, empathy and a sense of the sanctity of life fall foul of the culture of

> trivialisation in its exploitative dramas . . . Culture turns a blind eye to those who, once in power, use violence and exclusion to maintain their position and wealth. There is also an acceptance and even an admiration of vengeful violence; for example, in some of Stephen King's novels, and in films such as *Death Wish*, *Rambo*, *Batman* and *Mad Max* and their sequels . . . Inter-male violence is thereby condoned and valued . . . The repeated observation of such scenarios is likely to affect people's views of the world and their internalised standards for behaviour. This is especially so if they have few alternative role models or few opportunities to gain control over economic resources. Hence these aggressive role models are likely to have a marked impact on younger males who are poor and who are constantly confronted by television advertising that shows them what they do not and cannot have. In my view, our culture is preoccupied with such violence, in part because of the enormous levels of social injustice we tolerate, and the costs imposed on being seen as less able and marginalised.

This brief discussion of male violence began with the notions of its absurdity and its intractability. Violence is not simply the result of unleashing destructive influences, it is also crucially influenced by the absence of those impulses, and characteristics that temper and hold them in abeyance. Male violence makes sense when examined in this context. As long as we collectively create a society that reduces the capacity for compassion and empathy in boys and young men, as long as we teach men that their value is in their ability to score over others, as long as we marginalise large groups of such young men, as long as we shame and punish those who show the beginnings of destructive behaviour in reaction to these influences, rather than create useful alternatives for rehabilitation, then male violence, instead of being absurd, is in fact a logical outcome and is to be expected.

The new men

This book has resolutely avoided some of the more trendy and fashionable notions about men. This decade has seen popular media setting out a different form of masculinity that has been termed 'the new man'. The main characteristic of the new man is that he is 'in touch with his feelings'. Such a banal and ultimately trivial view of the complex challenges facing men offers very little. I like Joseph O'Connor's humorous description in *The Secret World of the Irish Male*:

> For a start I have no problem at all with men being emotionally repressed. It all depends on the emotions we're talking about. Hatred, jealousy, paranoia, violence, are all well worth repressing. If male emotional repression means fewer men still beat up their wives, hey, I can live with that. Women should repress these emotions too in my book.
>
> But perhaps I am untypical too. The men I know are all 'new men'. They have read their Germaine Greer. They can watch those television advertisements for feminine hygiene products — with wings — without tittering, blushing or flapping their arms. The men I know are nurturing, kind, balanced, at one with their inner children, kind to stray puppies. They talk about their feelings all the time. Indeed the men I know seem to do nothing except talk about their bloody feelings. Me included. I often sense that the reason my women friends keep trying to get me drunk is that they want me to lighten up, stop droning on about Sylvia Plath's poetry and how awful PMT must be, and simper admiringly about football and supermodels instead.

While somewhat adolescent in tone this description fits the stereotype of the new man quite well. The decades of the eighties and nineties, grounded in some quite fantastic assumptions about the nature of gender, and a good deal of academic politically correct gyrations usually called 'gender studies', have produced an image of the new man. He is quite a sanitised version of the old 'warrior' patriarch type. He is an emasculated, sensitive, gentle, thoughtful and nurturing pacifist, who eats proper food (i.e. lots of salad). He is what one man interviewed recently in a documentary on the subject of men called an 'emotional transvestite'. He dresses up his emotional self as a woman. The new man is a creation of political and social mores. He is the 'Twiggy' of this male generation. And when we look more closely he is actually conspicuous by his absence. According to Ann and Bill Moir, in their excellent book *Why Men Don't Iron*, 'The New Man's most salient characteristic is his rarity. If he had feathers he would be an endangered species.'

A more recent version of the 'new man' is being put forward by the men's movement as a reaction to the rather feeble and timid version described above. Elements of the men's movement try to reclaim some of the primal qualities of masculinity and save them from the frilly-lined dustbin into which they have been discarded. Central to this attempt is the effort to help men discover their inner warrior, or wild man. While sympathetic to any cause that helps men realise that they are passionate and deeply emotional beings, I don't believe that this type of stereotyping is useful. Men do not need to reclaim some lumbering, half-developed inner Neanderthal in order to be fully male and fully human. They do need to respect their masculinity with all its beauty as well as its weaknesses, and seek to find ways to live well-balanced lives.

Another of the 'new man' ideologies tells us that all heterosexual men are trying to suppress their inner gay man. And the more intense the repression the more powerfully the gay man inside is pushing to get out. The new man is therefore bisexual, and his notion that he isn't is denial, usually identified by his tendency to be revolted at the idea of men having sex with each other. This view tells us that men are not only confused about their sexuality, but they are stupid.

Bisexual, emasculated and insipid on the one hand, gently tending the garden while his partner scores points on the Stock Exchange, or wild, somewhat blind and self-absorbed, roaring at the moon on a warrior weekend, seem to be the solutions much of the conflict about manhood has come up with thus far. Neither is particularly attractive to me, or to most men I know. I think it's time to forget about the new man. There is no such thing.

Getting old

One of the negative effects of male influence in our world is that there is no place for getting old. Becoming feeble, forgetful and weak are signs of failure for men. Confronting old age with dignity is, thus, very difficult for many. Coping with the losses that gradually invade as the ageing process moves inexorably onward leads many men to sadness and despair. World-renowned developmental psychologist Eric Erikson saw the challenge of old age as being one where the main task is to experience what he calls ego integrity instead of despair. By this he means that old age is accepted as a part of one's life, that it is marked by a sense of completion of life and that good memories and positive beliefs about the contribution of one's life ease the passage towards death.

The world we live in does little to support and assist men to have these gifts awaiting them as they get old. Many are lonely for human intimacy having been unable to build the bonds that could now sustain them when the challenge and distraction of work is no longer available. A great number find themselves at a loss because they have had no preparation for this stage of life. If more men are to experience ego integrity rather than despair in the final chapter of their lives they need to learn to get ready for getting old.

Financial institutions are particularly effective in telling people about preparing for one aspect of retirement in the way they market pension policies. And there is something to be learned from them. Their strategy is to get people to understand that they will need financial security when their earning capacity has left them. Financial security is, however, only one important element of preparation for getting old. What good is it to be financially secure when you are spiritually bankrupt, isolated, bored and lonely? And this is the fate of many.

What then is involved in preparing for getting old? What kind of spiritual pension are you saving for, what kind of emotional benefits are built into the plan? One key element seems to be the attitude one takes to the ageing process. As we have seen earlier, male conditioning leads many men to see getting old as a matter of defeat and failure. This attitude has to change. A beautiful and helpful resource on this topic is Mitch Albom's recent book *Tuesdays with Morrie*. This little gem is an account of the author's conversations with his professor during the final months of his mentor's life. One encounter examines the issue of ageing thus:

> 'Weren't you ever afraid to grow old?' I asked.
>
> 'Mitch, I *embrace* ageing.'
>
> Embrace it?
>
> 'It's very simple. As you grow, you learn more. If you stayed at twenty-two you'd always be as ignorant as you were at twenty-two. Ageing is not just decay you know. It's growth. It's more than the negative that you are going to die, it's also the positive that you *understand* that you're going to die, and that you live a better life because of it.'
>
> Yes, I said but if ageing were so valuable, why do people always say 'Oh if I were young again.' You never hear people saying 'I wish I were sixty-five.'
>
> He smiled. 'You know what that reflects? Unsatisfied lives. Unfulfilled lives. Lives that haven't found meaning. Because if you have found meaning in your life you don't want to go back. You want to go forward. You want to see more, do more. You can't wait until sixty-five.

> 'Listen. You should know something. All younger people should know something. If you are always battling against getting older, you're always going to be unhappy because it will happen anyhow.
>
> 'And Mitch?'
>
> He lowered his voice.
>
> 'The fact is *you* are going to die eventually.'
>
> I nodded.
>
> 'It won't matter what you tell yourself.'
>
> I know.
>
> 'But hopefully,' he said, 'not for a long, long time.'
>
> He closed his eyes with a peaceful look, then asked me to adjust the pillows behind his head. His body needed constant adjustment to stay comfortable. It was propped in the chair with white pillows, yellow foam, and blue towels. At a quick glance it seemed as if Morrie were being packed for shipping.

So it seems one's attitude to ageing is based firmly on the issue of meaning in life, and this issue has already been explored in chapter 12.

Another element that seems to be particularly relevant here is the concept of creating memories. If Erikson's model of ego integrity is a useful way at looking at being fulfilled in old age, then the memories one can reflect on are important building blocks. Using the metaphor of a spiritual/emotional pension, one might ask what memories are being stored up in a treasured casket, to be taken out again and again and enjoyed in the autumn years of life. Making memories can be an active and purposeful activity. An example from my own life helps to illustrate this.

One summer's day when my daughter Sarah was six years old

we were walking along the seafront. She looked beautiful in her summer dress and with her wavy fair hair. We bought two big ice cream cones, climbed on to two big rocks that looked across at the Clare hills and indulged ourselves. I thought it a very special moment and explained to Sarah that oftentimes we forget these kind of experiences once they are over. I explained that there is a place in our memory where we can put things and that we could both just close our eyes and put this memory there and it would last for ever. So we did. Years later we were driving out along the same seafront when we noticed an extraordinary sunset. On impulse I suggested that we go somewhere we could see it better so we drove three miles out to a small quiet beach. We sat out on the rocks and talked about the colours and the amazing way the clouds looked like islands in the water, and watched the sun go down. On the way back Sarah talked about her memory of seven years earlier, with our big melting ice creams and the Clare hills in the distance. When Sarah is eighty years old and I am dead and gone she will still have these memories to comfort her and gladden her heart. And she also knows now how to make memories.

So many men are caught up, living in unawareness and not applying much reflection to what their lives are about. And for many old age will be too late to make the changes. If we ask this question 'Do I want to remember this when I am old?' of much of what we do from day to day it could have the effect of changing the way we live.

Conclusion

Sitting here pondering the end of the book, I reflect on why I began it in the first place. Certainly the seed was sown by my friend Owen a couple of years ago. I knew then that I could not write with any confidence on the topic, as I had yet some distance to travel in looking at my own sense of being a man and how it fitted with so much of the sexual politics that is all around. Additionally, I had too reactive a position about men as I saw much that was damaging in them. In the intervening years I think I began to understand why men are the way they are, the engine that drives them and the tracks that we set up for their paths through life.

One of the abiding images in the arguments about gender is the notion of the glass ceiling. When we think of male influence in the world we have been encouraged to come to grips with this invisible partition that separates the male elite from the rest of the world. Yes, there is a male elite, those who swagger with their brandy and cigars above the glass ceiling, comparing the size of their respective bank accounts, cars, houses and all the other trappings of success, the symbolic laurels and accolades of the victors. They wield their power with confidence and arrogance and hope to God that they don't slip.

If, however, we can look up through the glass ceiling we can also look down to the glass cellar. There we see the millions of dead and maimed young warriors of this civilised millennium. Alongside them are the disenfranchised men who lived and live half-lives, filled with undiagnosed despair, failures in their own eyes, and shamed by the world, getting sick and dying early. The criminals connive and violate, and get what they can from their forays up from the cellar to the world where the vast majority of men live.

Between the glass ceiling and the glass cellar live the men who are the ordinary heroes. Men who are decent, hard-working, compassionate and concerned. Those who want their children to be safe and well, to thrive and be happy, those who stop to help the stranded motorist, who protect those they love to the point of death. Many are now struggling to come to terms with new definitions of how to be a good man. Most have the heart to do so, they just need to find the way. I hope this book is of some use in that most challenging and fulfilling of tasks.

Michael Hardiman
Galway 1999

Sources

Albom, M., *Tuesdays with Morrie: An Old Man, A Young Man and Life's Greatest Lessons*, Great Britain: Little Brown and Co. 1998

Archer, J. (ed.), *Male Violence*, London: Routledge 1994

Barille, E. and C. Laroze, *The Book of Perfume*, London: Abbeville Press 1995

Bassoff, E., *Between Mothers and Sons*, London: Piatkus 1998

Bly, R., *Iron John: A Book About Men*, Reading, Mass.: Addison Wesley 1990

Bly, R., *The Sibling Society: The Culture of Half-adults*, Middlesex: Hamish Hamilton 1996

Bordo, S., 'Feminism, postmodernism, and gender skepticism' in Linda J. Nicholson (ed.), *Feminism/Postmodernism*, London: Routledge 1990

Bradshaw, J., *The Family*, Florida: Health Communications 1988

Campbell, A. and S. Muncer, 'Men and the meaning of violence' in John Archer (ed.), *Male Violence*, London: Routledge 1994

Capra, F., *The Tao of Physics*, London: Flamingo 1992

Carver, R., *All of Us: The Collected Poems*, New York: Knopf 1998

Chapin, H., 'The Cat's in the Cradle', Story Songs 1975

Chodorov, N., *Feminism and Psychoanalytic Theory*, Oxford: Basil Blackwell 1989

Clark, K., *Civilisation*, London: BBC 1977

Conroy, P., *Beach Music*, London: Bantam 1995

Descartes, R., *The Philosophical Works of Descartes*, trans. E.S. Haldane and G.R.T. Ross, Cambridge University Press 1931 de Vries, J., *The Five Senses*, Edinburgh: Mainstream Publishing Company 1997

Dickson, A., *The Mirror Within*, London: Quartet Books 1985

Donne, J., *Selected Poetry*, London: Penguin 1975

Doty, W.G., 'Companionship thick as trees: our myths of friendship', *Journal of Male Studies*, vol. 1, no. 4, May 1993, pp. 359–82

Dousse, R.M., 'A survivor of the 1997 Luxor Massacre remembers', *Hello!*, no. 571, August 1999

Dworkin, A., *Intercourse*, New York: Free Press 1987

Dylan, B., 'Like a Rolling Stone' from the album *Highway 61 Revisited*, Sony Music

Erikson, E., *Childhood and Society*, London: Penguin 1987

Farrell, W., *The Myth of Male Power*, London: Fourth Estate 1994

Faulks, S., *Birdsong*, London: Vintage Press 1994

Frazier, C., *Cold Mountain*, London: Sceptre Books 1997

Freud, S., *The Standard Edition of the Complete Works of Sigmund Freud*, ed. J. Strachey, London: The Hogarth Press 1955

Gangstead, S.W., cited in 'The new flirting game', *Psychology Today*, vol. 32, no. 1, 1999

Gilbert, P., 'Male Violence: Towards an Integration' in John Archer (ed.), *Male Violence*, London: Routledge 1994

Gray, J., *Men are from Mars, Women are from Venus: A Practical Guide for Improving Communication and Getting What You Want in Your Relationships*, New York: HarperCollins 1993

Gray, J., *What Your Mother Couldn't Tell You and Your Father Didn't Know: Advanced Relationship Skills for Better Communication and Lasting Intimacy*, New York: HarperCollins 1994

Gurian, Michael, *Love's Journey: The Seasons and Stages of Relationship*, Dublin: Gill & Macmillan 1995

Hardiman, M., *Children under the Influence*, Cork: Paragon 1992

Hardiman, M., *Healing Life's Hurts*, Dublin: Gill & Macmillan 1997

Hardiman, M., *Addiction: The CommonSense Approach*, Dublin: Newleaf 1998

Hillman, J., *The Soul's Code: In Search of Character and Calling*, London: Bantam 1997

Irigaray, L., 'This sex which is not one' in *A Reader in Feminist Knowledge*, New York: Routledge 1991

Jaspers, K., *General Psychopathology*, trans. J. Hoenig and M. Hamilton, Manchester University Press 1963

Kafka, F., *The Trial*, London: Penguin 1987

Keane, J.B., *The Field*, Dublin/Cork: Mercier Press 1966

Keen, S., *Fire in the Belly: On Being a Man*, New York: Bantam 1991

Kierkegaard, S., cited in Ben Ami Scharfstein, *The Philosophers: Their Lives and the Nature of their Thoughts*, Oxford: Basil Blackwell 1980

King, S., *The Shawshank Redemption*, New York: Signet Books 1995

Lacroix, N., *The Scented Touch*, Oxford: Sebastian Kelly 1999

Levi, P., *If This is a Man*, London: Abacus 1987

Levi, P., *The Drowned and the Saved*, London: Michael Joseph 1988

Lewis, C.S., *The Abolition of Man*, Glasgow: Fount 1978

Marcel, G., *The Philosophy of Existentialism*, New Jersey: Citadel Press 1956

Maslow, A., *Motivation and Personality*, New Jersey: Van Norstrand 1967

Millet, K., *Sexual Politics*, New York: Doubleday 1970

Moir, Ann and Bill, *Why Men Don't Iron: The Real Science of Gender Studies*, London: HarperCollins 1998

Nietzsche, F., *On the Genealogy of Morals*, New York: Vintage 1969, cited in Susan Bordo, 'Feminism, postmodernism, and gender skepticism'

O'Connor, J., *The Secret World of the Irish Male*, Dublin: New Island Books 1994

O'Donohoe, J., *Anam Cara: Spiritual Wisdom from the Celtic World*, London: Bantam 1997

Pittman, F., 'Frank matters', *Psychology Today*, June 1998

Real, T., *I Don't Want to Talk About It: Overcoming the Secret Legacy of Male Depression*, Dublin: Newleaf 1997

Rogers, C., *On Becoming a Person: A Therapist's View of Psychotherapy*, Boston, Mass.: Houghton Mifflin 1961

Sharpe, T., *Wilt*, London: Pan 1975

Siegal, B., *Love, Medicine and Miracles*, London: Arrow 1989

Spielberg, W.E, 'Why men must be heroic', *Journal of Male Studies*, vol. 2, no. 2, 1993, pp. 173–89

Springsteen, B., 'Adam Raised a Cain' from the album *Darkness on the Edge of Town*, Bruce Springsteen 1978

Springsteen, B., 'The Human Touch' from the album *Human Touch*, Bruce Springsteen 1989

Stanway, A., *The Complete Book of Love and Sex*, London: Arrow 1989

Wilson, P., *The Little Book of Calm*, London: Penguin 1996

Winn, M., *Children without a Childhood*, London: Penguin 1983

Wolfe, T., *The Right Stuff*, London: Bantam 1983

Yalom, I., *Love's Executioner and Other Tales of Psychotherapy*, London: Penguin 1991